THE SONG OF THE POOR

AND OTHER STORIES OF
EL SALVADOR

TOMMY GREENAN

DARTON · LONGMAN + TODD

INTELLIGENT ◆ INSPIRATIONAL ◆ INCLUSIVE
SPIRITUAL BOOKS

First published in 2024 by
Darton, Longman and Todd Ltd
Unit 1, The Exchange
6 Scarbrook Road
Croydon CR0 1UH

© 2024 The estate of Tommy Greenan

The right of Tommy Greenan to be identified as the
Author of this work has been asserted in accordance with the Copyright,
Designs and Patents Act 1988

A catalogue record for this book is available from the British Library

ISBN 978-1-915412-38-6

Designed and produced by Judy Linard
Printed and bound in Great Britain by Bell and Bain, Glasgow

CONTENTS

Acknowledgements   7

Introduction   9

Tommy Greenan   15

The Earthquake in El Salvador   25

Sumpul de Avelares   28

Carolina   31

Rising from the Grave   32

Children of the War Zone   34

Weeping for Sion   36

Purple Flowers   38

Three Reflections on Mother Earth   39

Servant of the Sacred   41

Pablo   43

Sun Trek   45

Letter to Niña Francisca   47

Death's Door (Daniel, Part 1 of 3)   49

The Grave of a Young Rebel   51

El Imperialismo   53

Church of the Poor   54

The Poor with You always   56

Daniel Dastardly (Part 2 of 3)   57

Christmas Tears   59

Child of Epiphany   63

The Shadow of Reality   65

In Remembrance   67

Heaven's Wisdom   70
Paradise of the Poor   72
Adiós, Don Pablo   74
The Life of the Trees   76
A Child's Prayer   78
Child's Play   79
Halloween   80
Here Comes the Sun   83
Birthday Crackers   87
The Cross   90
The Subversion of the Gospel   92
Easter Bells   94
Paschal Fire   96
The Peace Proposal   97
The Death of a Mentally Retarded Child   101
Sunt Lacrimae Rerum   103
Little Francisco   105
Back to Square One   107
The Song of the Poor   109
The Death of Christ   111
Sonya   113
Queen of the Road   115
The Wound of Loss   116
What the Dickens   118
Banter   120
Give Sorrow Words   123
The Sons of Cain   125
Doggy Go Home   127
A Candle for Chico   128

An Emmaus Walk	130
To the Thorn-Crowned Christ	131
The Tenth Anniversary	132
The Winds of Conflict	134
Golgotha	136
Tito el 'Bolo'	137
The Valley of the Fallen	139
Tito's Thank You	140
Las Chicas	141
Roses	143
Premature Pardon	144
The Tale of the Water Tap	146
The Murder of a Son	148
You're Sweet	151
Grief Work	155
The Ravages of War	157
On Scholastic Certainties	160
Grab the Bull by the Tail	161
Things Bright and Beautiful	164
The Mother Child	167
A Leap in the Dark	168
A Lesson too Late	169
The Army Death Squads	170
The Flight of a Captive Bird	172
Incest	174
The Nightmare	176
The Cross and the Earthly Banner	177
Somos Una Sombra	179
The Unfinished Symphony	183

Not Me, My Dear   185

The Casting of the Curse   186

Demobilised   187

A Crippled Old Man   190

A Parting Gift   193

A Dream Inviting Regeneration   197

The Village Almond Tree   199

Ode to a Fat Rat   200

The Struggle for Peace   201

Félix's Final Journey   205

Adiós, Daniel Dastardly (Part 3 of 3)   207

'¿Quién Como Dios?'   208

ACKNOWLEDGEMENTS

A SURPRISINGLY LARGE GROUP of people has been involved in helping to prepare this book by Father Tommy Greenan for publication. The main driving force behind the project, circulating Tommy's writings in draft, recruiting people to help with different stages of the process and tirelessly moving things forward, has been Henry McLaughlin, the priest who worked alongside Tommy in El Salvador at the time when the pieces were written. Henry has been supported in this throughout by Tommy's large extended family, particularly his brother, Joe Greenan; and by one of Tommy's lifelong friends, Jim McKelvie. Tommy didn't have access to a typewriter and his El Salvador pieces were written on loose sheets of paper. Sporadically he posted them to friends and family, and only many years later did they come to be known about by most of those who knew him. The major job of typing them up was then meticulously done by Pat (Patricia) Shearer.

Some time after embarking on the publication project, Henry was put in touch (through mutual friends Brother John Halsey and Mignon Ling), with an editor who formerly worked with the Scottish publisher Birlinn Ltd, Tom Johnstone. Tom advised on publishing matters, and took on the task of copy-editing the whole of *The Song of the Poor* and setting it in page proof, so it could be circulated to interested parties in a more conventional form than as typewritten sheets.

Once Tommy's writings had been put into book form, the entire text was proofread by Henry and by Jim and Mary McKelvie. Henry then commissioned the journalist Father Alcides Ernesto Herrera Guevara to write an introduction explaining the El Salvador background, and this was translated from the Spanish for this edition by Jim and Mary McKelvie.

Gordon Hunter provided legal advice and a host of others have freely offered support to the publication plans and read parts or all of *The Song of the Poor*. Some have provided photographs used in this edition. Those who have helped in these ways include various members of Tommy's family; Lilian Marina Andino; Christopher Binns; Daniela Denyse Brunet; Ann Burnet; Dave Connarty; Pauline Connarty; John Dalton; Maureen Douglas; Julian Filochowski; Brother John Halsey; Richard Holloway; Fintan Hurley; Paul Laverty; Mignon Ling; Mick McCaughan; Tim McConville; the Rev. Dr John McCulloch; Sheila McCullough; Dr Ian McDonald; Geraldine McKelvie; Rosa Murray; Maria Tippett.

For an unusual project like this, it was something of a challenge to find a literary agent with the nerve and insight to take it on – Piers Blofeld of Sheil Land was the agent who rose to the challenge.

An illustrated Spanish-language edition, *El Canto del Pueblo Pobre*, has already been published in El Salvador by Equipo Maiz. Equipo Maiz, established in 1983, is noted for its books analysing Salvadoran and Central American politics, economics, and society, and for its commitment to the Church of the Poor which is now being prioritised by Pope Francis. Many friends of Tommy and Henry generously helped to make the Equipo Maiz edition possible.

INTRODUCTION
by Fr Alcides Ernesto Herrera Guevara

FOR MORE THAN A hundred years in El Salvador an oligarchy, comprising some 14 powerful families who shared political power with the military, imposed an economic model and dictatorship on the population which, with the direct and indirect support of successive US governments, kept the country in a state of intense and bloody civil war.

From 1880 to 1980, the history of El Salvador was marked by the struggle of the peasants for land, frustrated attempts at agrarian reform and military repression. On top of this, political control was held by the military, whose position was secured as a result of coups d'états and fraudulent elections.

The first significant social uprising was silenced in 1932 and resulted in ethnic cleansing. Historical studies show that between ten thousand and thirty thousand indigenous peasants were murdered under the regime of the dictator Maximiliano Hernández Martínez.

In the 1960s, a new movement against the repression began. Educational organisations, peasants, labourers, public sector workers and others confronted the regime. These years of social unrest culminated at the end of the 1970s in a popular war for the liberation of the people, which took the form of insurgent groups against the Salvadorean army. Popular organisations had lost all hope of change and reform by democratic means. Two major electoral frauds, one in 1972 and the other in 1977, had shown that the electoral route was impossible. In the face of a dissenting population who rejected them completely, the military and oligarchy would come to stage another coup d'état in 1979.

At the beginning of the 1980s, 75 per cent of the land was in the hands of the oligarchy. A huge peasant body was enslaved, and the rest of the citizens were subjected to police laws such as that of vagrancy. In force since 1879, this law subjected them to forced labour on ranches.

In these circumstances, the life of the people as told by Father Tommy Greenan unfolds amidst great shortages such as a lack of education, healthcare, food, shelter, work and clothing. It would seem as if, in these 100 years from 1880 to 1980, life had come to a standstill. Modernisation only reached certain sectors. In 1985, for example, firewood was still the source of energy used by 74 per cent of the population.

The Song of the Poor is a description of the daily life in rural areas and of the peasantry in the 1980s. The streets of the villages, and even the towns, were dusty in summer and became a quagmire in winter. Very few vehicles made their way along rural roadways, except when the Army or some local landowner passed by. The passing of a vehicle was signalled by the howling of dogs rather than the noise of the engine. The peasant population travelled along these roads on foot, on horseback or in carts.

Most of the dwellings were made from adobe (mud and grass bricks dried in the sun), from bahareque (wood, stone and mud) or from wood and straw. Nearly all the homes had dirt floors, no electricity and were lit with beeswax candles or small homemade paraffin oil lamps. The house served as a store for each household's year's supply of maize corn and for sleeping at night. The roof jutted out a few feet over the front wall of the house. This open-air space provided shade where family members could rest on a bench or in a hammock. The women did the cooking in an outdoor shelter. The hallway of the house was where the family gathered. What we would call the living room was the bedroom for the men, where the hammocks were strung up.

Life in the country started very early. At four in the morning, the woman of the house was first to rise. She had to prepare a breakfast meal for 'the men of the house' so that they could take it to work if this was far off or, on the other hand, she would have to take it along herself to the workplace at seven in the morning. Those whose task it was to work on the land started at four in the morning and finished at twelve midday. In the afternoon, the men spent their time tending their own crops, playing football or gambling with other neighbours. The women were first to get up in the morning and last to go to bed, as well as having to leave everything clean and prepared for the following day.

Rural community life centred on domestic chores, crops, religion, football and drinking. But, most of all, it was engaged in the struggle for survival in the face of food shortages, illnesses, alcohol addiction and war. One day a week was set aside for 'going into town'. Some went to sell their wares, others to Mass and the majority to buy things they couldn't make at home.

Death was a daily reality. It demanded a religious ritual of prayer during the wake, then for the following nine days. Later, there would be another ritual lasting forty days, and then another until the memorial of the first anniversary. Wakes were marked by a meal of maize corn *tamales*, homemade liquor and prayers. As part of their routine almost every day, the women of the communities had to attend the praying of the rosary for some deceased person or other.

In order to understand the stories narrated by Father Tommy Greenan, it's necessary to understand the position of the Church and the role priests played in rural areas and in major conflict zones of the Civil War.

After the meetings of Latin American bishops in Medellín (1968) and Puebla (1979), progressive priests changed their method of evangelisation. In Latin America most priests have parishes of thousands of parishioners, many have tens of thousands and Fr Greenan's colleague, Fr Henry McLaughlin, himself lived for a few months in one where there were 75,000 parishioners and the priest in the neighbouring parish had over 100,000. Many parishes were composed of villages very dispersed in mountains and jungle, making travel slow and difficult.

These conditions led to the growth of the Comunidades Ecclesiales de Base movement, usually translated as Basic Christian Communities (BCC). However 'de base' actually means grassroots. To convey to English speakers what the name means, a better translation is Grassroots Christian Communities. The Grassroots Christian Communities movement, in which small groups of Christians were formed within parishes, became one of the focal points of pastoral action. This involved the laity looking at the reality, judging the situation in the light of the Word of God and Church doctrine, and acting to transform this reality. In this sense the BCC stirred a sense of justice in the people, making them conscious of the oppression which had been suffered, and gave thousands of peasant men and women the incentive to mobilise themselves.

Gathered in their groups, the people came to understand better the teaching of Jesus, and they allowed it to deepen their faith and change their lives. From them comes a new way of following Jesus and a new way of understanding, which then with the help of academics is explored in books of Liberation Theology (a theology from and for oppressed and exploited people). This is sometimes referred to as a new theology and a new way of being Church. It is radical in the sense it is going back to the roots, and in its practice is very similar to that of Gospel times and the early Christians. It meant that in the parishes, many went from being part of groups with devotion to the Sacred Heart to becoming members of FECCAS (Christian Federation of Salvadorean Peasants).

Probably since Constantine, the Catholic Church has acted from the top down. Grassroots Christian Communities work from the bottom up. This change is now reflected in the actions and words of Pope Francis.

Father Greenan's pastoral work was in a place where military repression was permanent and cruel. Priests were considered subversives – 'red priests' – who encouraged insurgence with their preaching and working practices. This made them targets for attack by government forces. In a most notorious incident on 16 November 1989, six Jesuit priests who had sided with the poor against the military dictatorship, along with a housekeeper and her daughter, were murdered by members of the Atlacatl Battalion, an elite unit of the Salvadoran army. Every time he set foot outside the Parish House Father Greenan was putting his life at risk. Not only did he consider himself obliged to go out to celebrate Mass, but also perhaps to take a pregnant woman or a child with diarrhoea to the clinic. Or he might go to help peasants transport their agricultural products or celebrate a funeral with them or to take them to an army barracks in search of a family member who had been detained or a son who had been kidnapped with the aim of forcing him to enlist for military service.

These stories demonstrate that reality. On the one hand we have a priest who knows and lives a reality amongst the poor people, full of sadness, of pain, but also full of hope and the struggle for justice. On the other hand, he describes to us as an outsider how he perceives the reality lived by the Salvadorean peasant in diverse circumstances at a given moment in history.

This pastoral experience of Father Greenan is written from the standpoint of 'the preferential option for the poor' (Puebla 1979), and draws on the philosophy and pastoral work of Archbishop Romero, saint and martyr. Romero had been nominated Archbishop of El Salvador in 1977, and for the next three years he sided with the poor and the victims of state repression, denouncing the abuse of their human rights by the rich and powerful. For this he was assassinated – shot by a sniper at the altar as he celebrated mass on 24 March 1980. He had preached that the pastor should be found wherever there is suffering (30 October 1977).

The stories recount events such as earthquakes, war, daily life, religion, the beliefs and traditions of the people amongst other things. In other words Father Greenan presents us with a vision from *Gaudium et Spes*, the document from the Second Vatican Council (1962-65) which defined the Church's response to the problems of the modern world – 'The joys and the hopes, the griefs and the anxieties of the men of this age, especially those who are poor or in any way afflicted, these are the joys and hopes, the griefs and anxieties of the followers of Christ. Indeed, nothing genuinely human fails to raise an echo in their hearts.'

The 92 stories of *The Song of the Poor* reveal the real humanity of a pastor at the heart of a little town and its surrounding villages in the mountains of Chalatenango, suffering the same repression, feeling the same pain, but bringing hope. Aptly, in the first piece about the earthquakes and reflecting on the war, Father Greenan describes it exactly:

> We shouldn't look to God as the Power behind the earthquake (in the supernatural). Rather, the God of Jesus Christ is among the dead, the wounded and those afflicted by the earthquake in El Salvador. God is not a distant power. God is present in the crucified and broken of El Salvador.
>
> As far as the Civil War is concerned: this will only end when this vicious spiral of repression and injustice, which holds the majority prisoner in material and spiritual poverty, is permanently abolished once and for all.
>
> (Greenan, 12 October 1986)

This presence of God in the crucified people which we encounter in *The Song of the Poor* is also a demonstration of the solidarity, filled with mercy, of those pastors who are faithful to the Gospel. Each experience recorded in his stories shows us Father Greenan listening to the clamour of the poor people and being affected by it. Once again we see in this the pastoral embodiment of the words of the martyred bishop: 'the face of Christ among sacks and baskets, the face of Christ amongst the torture and mistreatment in the prisons, the face of Christ dying of hunger in the children who have nothing to eat.' (Archbishop Romero, 26 November 1978)

The Song of the Poor is an account of the lives of the poor and the suffering in El Salvador in the historical context of earthquakes and civil war, with the intervention of the United States government. This is the life that Father Greenan puts to music. His stories strike different notes. Just like a melody, with its sharps and flats, so the life of the Salvadoran people plays out in every tale.

TOMMY GREENAN

FR THOMAS GREENAN (TOMMY) was born on 20 January 1956 in Edinburgh, and baptised at St Theresa's in Craigmillar. He was one of ten children and is survived by four brothers and four sisters.

He was educated at St Francis' Primary School in Craigmillar, then St John's in Portobello, before attending the junior seminaries St Vincent's, Langbank (1968-70), and Blairs College near Aberdeen (1970-74). He then studied for the priesthood at the Scots College in Valladolid from 1974 to 1980 and was ordained at St John's in Portobello in July 1980.

Tommy Greenan served Holy Cross Parish in Edinburgh (1980-81) and St Andrew's, Livingston (1981-86).

He was on mission in El Salvador from 1986 to 1994 and 1996 to 2001 and shared in the poverty of the communities there. He had moved to El Salvador joining fellow Edinburgh priest, Fr Henry McLaughlin, living and working in the area of Chalatenango, at the time a conflict zone. This was in the years following the 1980 assassination of Óscar Romero, the then Archbishop of San Salvador, whose life and work inspired Fr Greenan to write a thesis, later published as a book, on his homilies.

He attended Comillas University in Madrid from 1994 to 1996. His Master's thesis *Archbishop Romero's Homilies: A Theological and Pastoral Analysis* was published in Spanish before being translated and published in English in 2018. As well as the homilies, the book covers the life of Óscar Romero, his teachings and the role of the Church in El Salvador. Tommy said at the time: 'It is great to know this book can now be read by many more and I hope those that do enjoy this analysis of Óscar Romero's homilies.' Bishop Toal wrote the foreword to the English edition and said: 'Tommy was idealistic and very clever with words – he had a poetic spirit in him.'

He had returned to Spain for further studies from 2001 to

2005, and there completed his doctorate in Spanish on the life and work of Romero.

After many years with the poor in El Salvador, Tommy decided to try pastures new. In 2005 he returned to Central America, this time to work with Mayan Indians in Peten, Guatemala. This was in line with his choice to be with the poorest, the most suffering.

Following a military coup engineered by the CIA in 1954, Guatemala had descended into a nightmarish chaos in which the slaughter of the indigenous Mayan population by the Guatemalan military was an everyday occurrence. In 1985 Noam Chomsky described the country as 'a literal hell-on-earth, which has been maintained by regular US intervention until today'. In 1998, the Guatemalan Bishop Gerardi and his team published a report based on thousands of testimonies and years of research, documenting more than 400 massacres of Mayan Indians, nearly all committed by the Guatemalan Army, and resulting in more than 200,000 deaths. This was in effect a genocidal campaign aimed at eliminating the Mayan population. Two days after the publication of the report, Bishop Gerardi was bludgeoned to death in his home by two Army officers.

This was the country into which Tommy had come. The years that followed were difficult for Tommy. Brilliant at languages, he was confident he would soon be speaking a Mayan language. But he hadn't taken into account the truth that the younger we are the easier it is to learn. Now his memory was betraying him. He was brilliant in Spanish but he was unable to communicate with the Indians in their own language. The Indian world, their culture, spirituality and religious practices were all new to him. A very shy and introverted personality, Tommy was isolated and didn't have the backup and the opening of doors he had found in El Salvador. In El Salvador friends like the Irish Franciscans opened doors for Tommy and his fellow priest Henry McLaughlin. The poor knew the Franciscans and knew that on their recommendation they could trust the Scottish priests. Particularly in a war situation, it was great for priests to have people they could relax and have a beer with, and who with difficult problems could talk openly and seek the best course of action. In his new parish there was no one to tell the Indians Tommy was on their side. In a place like Petén, trusting the wrong person could cost you your life.

Not too long after Tommy had completed his doctorate, dementia crept in. This made him even more vulnerable. He was stubborn and turned a deaf ear to family and friends telling him it was time he returned permanently to Scotland. Then, in 2011, a small army of gunmen arrived in buses and attacked workers on a coconut farm in his parish of Petén, which was close to the Mexican border. The area had become increasingly dangerous as Mexican drug smugglers extended operations into Central America to escape a crackdown at home. The attack was carried out by 200 gunmen, who killed 25 men and two women, all of whom were decapitated.

Tommy saw the beheaded bodies of the victims, who were probably his parishioners. It traumatised him, distressed him each time he remembered it to the day of his death. Following this event, and a robbery that left him penniless, he eventually accepted he had to go home. However, he was in a very bad state and got totally lost and disorientated on the journey back. He turned up in Madrid, confused and homeless, before his friends and family brought him back to Scotland.

Once back home, thanks to his brother Joe and Joe's family, Tommy recovered a lot. His mother had suffered with dementia. Tommy had a great fear of it, but its progress was relentless. Many in Scotland loved and cared for Tommy, in particular the domestic staff at Gillis, the Archdiocesan Centre, the nuns and staff of St Joseph's Gilmore Place Care Home and the staff of St Margaret's Care Home in Edinburgh.

Tommy Greenan died peacefully on Sunday 17 May 2020 at St Margaret's Care Home in Edinburgh. He had been suffering from Alzheimer's and was 64 years old.

His brother Joe said: 'He saw some horrific things in Latin America. But even though he was on the other side of the world he was always there for me. He was gentle and kind and I've never seen my mother so proud as at Tommy's ordination. When I last saw him yesterday [Sunday 17 May], I told him: "I could live a million lives and could still never repay you for what you've done for me."'

Bishop Joseph Toal, of Motherwell Diocese, visited Tommy Greenan in El Salvador in 1999 on a trip organised by SCIAF. He said: 'When Óscar Romero was murdered that made a big impression on Tommy and was one of the things about him going to El Salvador. He integrated into these communities and shared their lifestyle. That perhaps took a toll on him – it was a Spartan life.'

Bishop Toal remembered Tommy as a determined character and a gifted footballer when they both attended junior seminaries and later the Scots College in Valladolid. 'He did Spanish at Blairs [College] and read a lot of Spanish literature, so when we went to seminary in Spain he was far ahead of me! I got to know him well there and we were ordained within days of each other. When Tommy wanted to do something he gave himself to it 100 per cent – he was very single-minded. My thoughts and prayers are with his family.'

He added: 'One of the things I remember was him getting up early every day to go the chapel and read the Bible through from start to finish. He was also an excellent footballer and supported Hibs. He was very keen on the Church in Latin America, and with his strong background in Spanish, he wanted to go there after he was ordained.'

Tommy Remembered by Fr Henry McLaughlin

In 1985 Tommy expressed his desire to work as a missionary in El Salvador. By then I had been three years in Latin America. When I volunteered I never dreamt that others from Scotland might want to do the same. Tommy was the second of four of us from our Scottish Archdiocese. If I had had a profile of the ideal candidate for new volunteers, Tommy would not have fitted it.

On a preliminary visit his arrival in El Salvador was a

baptism of fire. At that time I was helping the Franciscan Fathers Brendan Forde and John Dalton (who was on holiday in Ireland). It was a very tense and difficult time and 164 civilian survivors of a military death squad had fled their Guazapa mountain villages and were seeking protection inside our church in the very small town of Carrizal. Two babies had been born during the survivors' fourteen-day flight from the army. Their ages ranged from 7 days to 83 years. They told us their story of loved ones being murdered. Tommy spoke Spanish. He understood everything they said.

With good reason the local people were crying. They feared that the government who were targeting the Guazapa people would send planes to bomb Carrizal and all who lived there. Tommy was horrified at the ongoing suffering of the people who had chosen to seek asylum with us. He exploded, berating me and Father Brendan for showing no understanding or concern for the great danger the people were in. But his anger was misdirected. He didn't know that this was not our first meeting, and that the people had chosen to seek asylum with us. They knew that we would do everything we could to help them. Tommy's passion for those who were suffering at times revealed itself in visceral outrage. His instinctive impulse at times hurt people. It was a weakness he regretted.

It is only very recently that I have learnt things which help me better understand Tommy. He spent the first five years of his life in Craigmillar. It was one of the poorest areas of Edinburgh. He was very shy, introverted and sensitive. Aged twelve, he left home to go to the junior seminary in the west of Scotland. He wept when he left his mother and wept again every time he had to return to the seminary. Throughout his years at junior and later at senior seminary in Spain he struggled with the restrictions of a system determined to produce a model that denied his own strong values and identity.

He had a healthy resentment of the imposed rigid community structures of the seminary. As a seminarian in Spain he enjoyed the company of his fellow Spanish students and University professors, and found the humility and anti-clericalism of the Augustinian priests a breath of fresh air. But he was very nearly expelled for rebelling against the restrictions of seminary life.

Given his vulnerable nature and his resentment of authoritarian regimes, it was quite remarkably courageous that Tommy should choose to go to war-torn El Salvador in the 1980s. This was a military regime that murdered eighteen of our fellow priests in thirteen years, a government that distributed leaflets with the words – 'BE A PATRIOT! KILL A PRIEST!' Tommy channelled his righteous anger in his passionate efforts to ease the unjust suffering imposed on the poor. His own vulnerability allowed him to recognise the suffering of others.

I think the saying 'He can't see the forest for the trees' applies to Tommy. He was often blind to the bigger picture, but he was sensitive and observant to the small and the unnoticed. The little sapling merits our attention. It's so easy to miss things – to not notice people, or not take note of what's happening for them. One of the things we learn about Jesus is that he notices people whom others overlook. I'm sure you can remember people like Zacchaeus in the tree, or the leper he cured, or the woman at the well. He notices their pain, their isolation, their disease, and what's more he sets out to do something about it.

A few months after his first visit, Tommy returned and Archbishop Rivera decided that we two should together look after the villages of a parish in the hills of Chalatenango. At that time the activity of the government death squads meant that many of the villages of San Francisco Morazán parish had been destroyed, and the parish was geographically divided. Our main base was in the lower hills and the most distant village there was a two-and-a-half hour hike.

The nine villages in the higher hills were much more distant. Valle de Jesús was about a thirteen-hour hike away. Avelares was the nearest, about five hours away. However, four of those hours were through the de-populated wooded hills and a recognised free-fire zone. Only if you were tired of living would you wander off the dirt road.

During this time I came to know Tommy as vulnerable, sensitive, generous and occasionally explosive. He was a man of great humility. But his humility went out of the window when talking of his soccer prowess! He loved soccer and was a skilful player for more than 40 years. Both of us enjoyed the hiking we had to do visiting our villages. This included getting to our village of Yerba Buena near the top of Cerro Negro, a mountain of more than 6,000 feet. Tommy enjoyed nature. He would whistle at the birds, and they whistled back.

We live in a world where many want more and more. Tommy was a bit uncomfortable when he had money. He seemed happier without it. He lived frugally and was generous to the needy. He was reluctant to spend money even on decent footwear. Most of the time in our remote parish we had no access to electricity or a phone and he wouldn't even buy himself a transistor radio. Eventually, he got the gift of one and thoroughly enjoyed it. He did, however, spend money on books. He was an avid reader. As well as studying the Bible and scholarly theological tomes, he enjoyed literature.

Unknown to me, during our years together in Salvador Tommy wrote hundreds of these marvellous reflections/stories. Their focus was not on himself, but on the poor and needy. An example of his humility is his underestimation of the quality of his writing. If these stories were mine I would have had them published 25 years ago.

Tommy's writings make me think of the parables. In the story of the rich man and Lazarus (Luke 16:19–31), Jesus tells his audience – his disciples and some Pharisees – of the relationship, during life and after death, between an unnamed rich man and a poor beggar named Lazarus. In this story Lazarus is named, while the rich man remains anonymous. In a world where richness and fame are synonymous, and the poor are nameless and have no status, Jesus offers us an alternative story. In his parable Jesus has given to the whole world the poor man's name and tells his story of hell on earth, and how Lazarus is now with Abraham in Heaven. Tommy is doing the same, he is giving us the names of the poor and telling us their story. They are not nobody.

Above all, Tommy was a man of truth. When Tommy discovered an injustice his first instinct was to loudly denounce it. When I tried to urge him to be prudent his standard reply was: 'But it's the truth.' He wrote his University thesis on the homilies of Óscar Romero, the martyr-bishop who gave his life working for truth and justice in El Salvador. In the final pages of his book, *Archbishop Romero's Homilies: A Theological and Pastoral Analysis*, Tommy writes:

> The key to Romero is in his option for the poor. Their affliction tore open his heart . . . He was moved by entering into direct contact with the poor and came out bravely in their defence. He had compassion for them . . . With metaphors and popular idiom within the reach of the most humble . . . his theology was directed to the poor themselves, for the most part unable to read and write, as his privileged recipients.

Here Tommy is writing of Romero, but he is also revealing aspects of himself.

While we were two very different people, Tommy and I made a good team. The key was we both had a concern for the poor, and Tommy had a good heart. Both of us could say that our years working in El Salvador gave us the happiest days of our lives. Reading his writings enables me to recall and relive our time with the campesinos of El Salvador.

Gracias, Tommy.

Henry

1986

THE EARTHQUAKE IN
EL SALVADOR
12th October 1986

SITTING IN OUR PARISH house (which is about three hours'
bus journey from the city of San Salvador), we were surprised by
a sudden, violent movement which shook the building. It lasted
from three to five seconds but caused no apparent damage. The
electricity cut off immediately, and a child in the street outside
wept aloud. Besides the child's weeping all was silent.

Taking precautions, Fr Henry McLaughlin and I walked out
of the house. It was 11.50 a.m. on Friday, 10th October. In the
afternoon I travelled from our hill-country parish by bus and made
for the city. A section of the damage caused by the earthquake
could be seen as the bus passed by. People were standing helpless
at the side of the road, mattresses and other possessions stacked
high. Their adobe-mud dwellings had crumbled. Those living in
wooden, corrugated-tin shacks had no chance of withstanding the
blow either; they too were homeless. Telephone poles pulled
from the earth, shrubs, displaced soil and debris were strewn
along the roadway.

A volcano called San Jacinto wanted to erupt, tried, failed,
and the blockage caused the earthquake. Apparently, its eruption
had been predicted by seismologists three months ago. It was
reported in the newspaper *El Mundo*. Two other papers (*Prensa
Gráfica* and *El Diario*) accused *El Mundo* of scaremongering. They
continue to argue against the eruption of San Jacinto. However, if
San Jacinto does erupt, it will follow the same line of devastation
as the earthquake, biting through the centre of El Salvador, but
this time it will cause severe flooding in its wake.

The part of Soyapango where I'm lodging is outside the direct
line of the earthquake, but we suffered strong tremors throughout
Friday and Saturday night. I slept indoors. Most Salvadoreans in
our street preferred to bed down outside; even if their houses

were still intact, they didn't want to chance fate.

I've never experienced an earthquake before, but it's a strange sensation lying in bed during the night and hoping the ceiling doesn't fall down on you. On a few occasions the bed started to rock back and forward as if being pushed and pulled by some mischievous ghost. I suppose it would be an experience akin to finishing off a bottle of Johnnie Walker on your own, only this was happening outside the head . . .

The earthquake victims who survived are now homeless, hungry, lacking water facilities and, ironically, at the mercy of the heavy, tropical rains which usually fall in the afternoon. Many people have been killed by collapsed buildings. How many? We don't know yet. The government authorities don't want to cause panic, and the radio stations keep plugging 'I'm safe' messages from people in San Salvador to their loved ones in other parts of the country. Broken telephone cables are making communication difficult, causing even more worry and confusion.

Passing by Peel Children's Hospital by bus yesterday I could see the flat roof of a building which had come down like a sandwich, almost squeezing its way to the floor.

On a news bulletin our young, ultra-conservative, auxiliary Bishop Goyo Rosa stated with a melodramatic, quasi-apocalyptic, air that this happening was a sign from God that the country's civil war must end.

I disagree with his theology and I'm dubious of his politics. Firstly, God is not a capricious idol who whizzes down to earth from a supernatural sphere and causes this or that to happen. We need to have more respect for the transcendence of God. God is only present as the suffering, crucified One in our world. It's wrong to adopt in our age a pre-scientific, Old Testament or 'Primary Cause' interpretation of the reality we live. That's to say, we should not attribute to God direct, whimsical interventions into our history. Nature must run its course; evolution must take its toll. God, however, remains present in the world through the crucified people of history. God is incarnate in the dispossessed and trampled. Consequently, God does not intervene with displays of power in world events, butting in from the 'outside' (the 'supernatural'). Put quite simply: I believe that when it rains, God is not making water . . . We ought not to attribute directly to God that which runs according to the mysterious forces and energies in nature.

Monseñor Rosa should not be looking for God as the Power outside the earthquake (in the 'supernatural'). Rather, the God of Jesus Christ is in the dead, the wounded, the bereaved of the Salvadorean earthquake – not a Power apart. God is only present in the crucified and broken ones of El Salvador.

And as for the civil war: that will only end when this vicious spiral of repression and injustice which keeps the majority imprisoned in material and spiritual misery is once and forever abolished. Until then, it is better not to speak of God, earthquake and war in one sentence. The reality is too deep. Perhaps in these circumstances, it's better to hold counsel and keep silence.

SUMPUL DE AVELARES
12 November 1986

THIS MORNING I ROSE at about 6.30 a.m. and went outside into the daylight. A bullet had chipped the lintel, about two yards from where I was standing. I was questioned by one soldier, then on leaving the village, a group of them stopped me and took me behind the church, out of sight of the villagers.

They were quite gruff and one of them accused me of lying when I said I was the priest. He then helped himself to the contents of my belt-pouch after getting a mate to cover me with his rifle. He scrutinised my documentation and took note of my name and number of residence card. They found my detailed map with the markings of the places I was to visit and confiscated it. They radioed the High Command for them to check out with the Archbishop my possession of this map which interested and irked them.

Then, following the Jeff and Mutt routine, their leader apologised for the inconvenience and dismissed me with a veiled intimidation that they would come for me later on if they found it necessary to do so. I feel uneasy with my vulnerability.

But if I'm killed it'll be because I've sided with the down-trodden, and I will have died for the sake of downtrodden. Not, primarily, for the sake of Christ. Only secondarily for the sake of Christ, because he identified so completely with the downtrodden.

As I write, the hills continue to be bombed and machine-gunned from helicopters, and the people are 'afflicted' (as one woman put it) and the little children are frightened. I wish the United States government would stop providing weapons and machines for war. I wish the money allocated for this barbarity were given to save the lives of children suffering and dying from diseases which aren't fatal in the first world.

This evening, in the Eucharist, we read from Mark, chapter 4, where Jesus calms the storm and saves the lives of his frightened followers. The people of El Salvador are in the same situation, except it's not the waves of the sea, but the bombs of the air which menace.

1987

CAROLINA
January 1987, Chalatenango, El Salvador

I REMEMBER VAGUELY A poem we recited in class years ago. I can only remember one line: 'Lift her up tenderly, loving not loathing'. Maybe the poem is entitled 'Bridge of Sighs'. It's about the death of an unknown girl and the sadness this causes the poet.

I was visiting a family in Yerba Buena when they told me about Carolina. She was killed in mid-November 1986, as she fled from a surprise attack of soldiers. She fell dead on the dirt-track outside the family's house.

They say Carolina was a small girl. She was known as 'La Negrita' ('The Wee Dark One') because of her dark, Indian features. She would have been only slightly taller than the M16 rifle she lugged around with her. She was about sixteen years old when she died. It was a single army bullet that pierced her back and passed through her left breast. Yet, somehow, in a last, desperate lunge before she fell Carolina managed to toss her M16 rifle over the cliff-edge, foiling the enemy of a prize possession. This act of impish resistance forces a wry smile from the storyteller.

Carolina was very thin and rather frail. Only shortly before her death she had returned with the others from the taking of 'El Poy', a frontier army post. She was vomiting all the way back; nerves had got the better of her.

I look at her grave on the slope. A plank of wood jutting out of the soil gives leverage to her corpse. Silent beneath the dust and rocks, hidden by bushes, safe from the hungry pigs. She died young and she died poor.

'Guess you were never cut out for guerrilla warfare, Carolina. But what drove you to take this option? What cause did you find that was greater than life itself?'

I imagine the men of Yerba Buena lifting her remains, carrying her these ten yards to her final resting place. And the line of poetry echoes in my mind: 'Lift her up tenderly, loving not loathing'.

RISING FROM THE GRAVE
13th January 1987

I HAD NEVER CONDUCTED a burial like this before. The dead young man had been killed by a bullet wound to his left side. This happened in Santa Ana during the time of the coffee-picking. The Guerrilla, in their war tactic to ruin the economy, attacked government soldiers guarding the plantation. There was a crossfire and Jorge was shot dead.

We followed the coffin to the cemetery. I marvelled at the dignified restraint of the mourners. The composed, self-possessed wife carried a small pillow and cloth, and the reason for this baffled me. The grey coffin swayed and snaked its way forward, carried by pall-bearers who displayed signs of over-indulgence with the local firewater.

At the side of the open grave the deceased's brother conducted a drunken brawl with a youngster who tried in vain to pacify him. They rolled in the dust, fists flying, words slurred.

To cover the embarrassment, we thought it best to lower the coffin immediately and proceed with prayer. Jorge's wife interrupted, bringing forward the small pillow and cloth. She asked that the coffin lid be removed in order that she could lay the pillow beneath her deceased husband's head. I thought, Lord, he smelleth. Owing to the heat, decomposition of mortal remains is swift. For this reason, there is a glass peek-hole in the coffin lid to allow mourners to look in without taking off the lid. Jorge's wife stooped and looked through the peek-hole. She released a high-pitched wail. Other women joined her and orchestrated their grief.

A drunk tottered to the fore with a hammer and started to prise at the lid. An old woman expressed her reservations publicly. I agreed with her and suggested we lower the coffin, gently taking the wife aside.

When they began to lower, I foresaw what was about to

happen. The coffin tilted on the cords, twirled a half circle, and clattered face-down to the bottom of the grave. The wailing went into crescendo. The drunk culprits looked gormless. A sober young man jumped down and twisted the coffin upright. It was a comedy of errors although nobody was laughing. He couldn't get out, so I extended my right hand and levered him to the surface. This was the only time I had ever raised anybody from the grave.

CHILDREN OF THE
WAR ZONE
February 1987

THE HELICOPTER'S ENGINE ROARS overhead. The 'avispita' ('little wasp') threatens to spit out its bullets and rockets among the surrounding hills as it patrols, hungry in search of the Guerrilla.

Looking anxious and needing reassurance little Nena says, 'Mummy, I'm scared of the wee wasps'. Her mother smiles. Nena voices everyone's feelings.

A rocket explodes against the sheer rock-face up above and bullets stutter out loudly. The avispita has spotted its prey. Ana Cecilia begins to cry tears of fear. I pick her up in my arms and she feels comforted and not so lonely and she stops crying.

Soon the Government troops occupy the village. They approach cautiously, very wary of a possible Guerrilla ambush. I sit in the schoolhouse porch and watch them gradually relax their guard and loiter around the people's houses, asking for tortillas.

Rosa Philomena comes and sits beside me on the school bench. Her chubby cheeks and head of curls reminiscent of the cherubim. She usually likes to giggle and play hopping games, letting the bare soles of her feet smack against the cement. She seems more subdued today. She senses the tense atmosphere and hears the menacing drone of the avispita in the sky. Rosa Philomena thrusts her cherubic cheeks to my ear and whispers: 'I'm going back to my house if that guerrilla goes away'. I look at the soldier sitting on the porch wall of her house and, with a smile, wonder if he would be flattered by Rosa Philomena dubbing him 'that guerrilla'.

A few hours later the go-ahead command is given over the military radio and the soldiers file out of the village, climbing into the hills. Tension disappears and tranquillity returns to Avelares. Things become normal again.

In the evening, as I go for a quiet stroll, another bare-footed, grubby youngster, about seven years of age, meets me on the dirt-track. He carries in his hand a toy – a green, plastic aeroplane. Its tail is broken off. Plastic propaganda toys were distributed by the soldiers on their Christmas-time operation. I ask the lad how he is. His face serious, he answers: 'Padrecito, they haven't killed me yet.'

WEEPING FOR SION
March 1987

DON HÉCTOR AVELAR PERSUADED me to accompany him
to Chacones, heading directly north from the village where we
live. At daybreak we set off together along the forbidden road,
where even angels fear to tread. And angels can pass unharmed
by the blast of landmines!

Don Héctor is just another number in the statistic of
displaced people in El Salvador, just another 'campesino' forced
from his house and small patch of land. The journey we were
making was to lead us through Tremedal, his birthplace, a land
for him filled with memories of life and love. Tremedal is now
desolate wasteland. Houses once filled with people are now
empty, broken shells overrun by weeds. Tremedal is a silent
tomb which holds no life, an aborted womb, void of all living
contact.

Suddenly, turning the corner, we came face to face with
a battalion of soldiers. A line of green, black-spotted uniforms
blended chameleon-like with the overgrowth. Laden with
rucksacks, rifles, grenades and bazookas they walked in silence.
Their silence owed more to fear of a Guerrilla ambush than
reverence for the remains of Tremedal. We joined the line and
walked on.

'Up there, on that hill, is where we work.' Don Héctor
corrected himself, 'where we used to work'. Next, we passed
the ruined church; sacredness profaned.

The Lieutenant examined my identity papers as we walked,
'so as not to waste time'. Needless to say, he was very suspicious
of this bearded foreign priest wandering around the conflict
zone. But Don Héctor and I parted company from them without
greater incident and waded through a tunnel of grass and shrubs.
The path, like the village, has not been used these last seven lean
years.

High up the hill we stopped for breath. Don Héctor gazed down below and pointed his finger. He said, 'There's where we used to live. Our house, our maize-field, our pastureland, everything we have is here. We've had nothing since we fled from the violence and death seven years ago. Nothing but pain and the yearning to return in peace. My wife and children and I were all born here. I'm getting old and want to return. I want to return, and if they killed me for being in Tremedal then I'd die humbly.' He remained silent. Then he added, 'It makes you want to weep, seeing it as it is now. Anybody in his right senses would have to weep.' His voice cracked and tears ran down his cheeks. Tears of sadness. Tears of captivity.

'By the rivers of Babylon we sat down and wept, remembering thee, Sion. Our captors asked us for songs, but how can we sing the song of the Lord on alien soil! If I forget thee, Jerusalem, let my right hand wither.' (Psalm 137)

PURPLE FLOWERS
May 1987

TIRED AND FEELING A need for inspiration I went to the Cathedral in San Salvador and sat down on the bench at the side of the tomb which contains the mortal remains of the Archbishop Óscar Arnulfo Romero.

Monseñor Romero was killed by an assassin's bullet as he celebrated the Eucharist on the evening of the 24th March 1980. 'The oppressors' killed him because he spoke out boldly in the name of God against the slaughter of defenceless people. 'The misery of the poor touches the very heart of God . . . I beg you, I implore you, I order you in the name of God, "stop the repression".'

The blood of Monseñor Romero, shed at the altar for the poor and oppressed, is the seed of freedom which, one day, will flourish in El Salvador.

His rectangular-shaped tomb is made of brick, coated with cement and cream-coloured paint. It is simple and humble, no great ornamentation, no great stateliness. Beside it women were kneeling for a long time, motionless, in prayer. Then an old man dressed in well-worn clothes shuffled forward, carrying in his hand a bunch of purple flowers. These he crammed into a tin at the base of the tomb. And then he walked away.

There was no need for long prayers or many words; these purple flowers were the old man's prayer. They were his silent homage to a prophet dearly loved by the defenceless. They also expressed a deep sadness for all innocent victims of violence. In a sense, the purple flowers of an old man were evoking the tears of El Salvador which had so burdened the heart of Monseñor Romero during the last three years of his life. These flowers were pleading to God for a just end to El Salvador's civil war and for the health and happiness of its people.

THREE REFLECTIONS ON MOTHER EARTH
May 1987

The Fruit of Mother Earth

Two small, barefooted, ragged dolls gave me a huge smile with their bad and broken teeth. 'Mum and Dad are just coming. They went to fetch potatoes and cabbages,' one of them said.

Israel and his wife arrived parched and perspiring. They had come from neighbouring Honduras, carrying their heavy sacks ten miles. 'You've got to watch how you go. It's near the cliff-edge and if you take a wrong step there's no return,' Israel informed me.

At the end of my visit he put four potatoes from his sack into a plastic bag and gave them to me. I felt humbled and deeply moved by this gesture of generosity. I could see Israel was poor and he was giving out of his poverty. These four heavy potatoes had come ten miles on his back, adding greatly to his sweat and toil.

I thanked him and returned two of them, claiming that two potatoes were enough for my supper.

That evening, as I ate fried potatoes, I felt deep appreciation of Mother Earth's humble fruit.

The Children of Mother Earth

Twice I slid on the pieces of rock strewn along the downward path and found myself sitting, like a clown, in the dust.

On reaching the mud hut I met two children in the garden. Solemn-faced they stared at me. Despite friendly words I couldn't elicit any communication from them. How would I feel if a Martian suddenly appeared in my back garden and spoke like E.T.?

The youngest – a grubby-looking toddler – struck a comical picture. She was ambling about in broken wellington boots ten sizes too big for her. Her green dirt-smudged tee-shirt covered only half her swollen, parasite-filled tummy, and the little lady revealed no shame at exposing her naked bottom. I sat on a tree trunk and watched little Eve toddle welly-booted past me, all the while glancing suspiciously at this strange E.T. figure who had invaded her time and space.

Looking through the unshuttered window of their house, I saw Eve's little sister lying naked on the bed. The bed-matting beside the baby was smeared with dried-in excrement. She was crying, as all babies do, but there was no one there to hold her and console her with a cuddle. Unheeded tears are the reality of El Salvador.

I walked on down the dirt-track to the last house on the hill. There I met the young mother of these three children. She was holding another of her offspring in her arms. I explained that I had visited her house and had met her other three children. She said, 'The baby suffers from cerebral paralysis.'

At the root of it is always the same story. The living conditions of El Salvador's children are miserable. Their prospects of a healthy future are very bleak. They're condemned from birth to dust, burning sun and slave-labour. Born poor, they'll live the hardships of the poor and they'll die the death of the poor.

The Agony of Mother Earth
In Los Planes, Chalatenango, on the 23rd April 1987, Baby David Salguera was sucking milk from his mother's breast. His mother and he were travelling on the back of a lorry. A Salvadorean air-force helicopter flying nearby machine-gunned the lorry. A bullet pierced little David as he sucked his mother's milk. He died instantly.

Mother Earth cries out in anguish and outrage to the heavens. And silence is the reply.

SERVANT OF THE SACRED
20th June 1987

NOT FOR THE FIRST TIME I found myself sitting, awaiting the arrival of Government troops on a military operation in the area. Eventually they arrived and hurried to take up defensive positions at strategic points of the village.

A few soldiers recognised me as the priest who had been celebrating the Eucharist with the people in the previous village the night before. They made overtures of conversation, realising that to display open hostility to the villages' 'Padrecito' doesn't help them win the minds and hearts of the people.

Apparently solicitous, one of them asked if the Guerrilla ever gave me any trouble. Rather than be blatantly honest and say the Guerrilla show me nothing but respect and courtesy, I gave him the stock reply: 'They know we're of the people and if they offend us, they offend the people.'

Cradling his machine gun, the young recruit nodded, 'That's good. There's only one true church – the Catholic Church . . . the Catholic Church is sacred . . .'

I cringed inwardly and said nothing. At times prudence is the better part of valour.

My memory involuntarily cast itself back two days before. While walking the muddy track I had met a group of five teenagers belonging to the Guerrilla. Dipping into the string bag I shared bone-hard biscuits with them and gifted an orange to the pretty young lady with the M16 rifle. Conversation flowed easily between us.

On taking leave of these young people, I felt a tinge of sadness. Death shadows their young lives. The Army was at that moment searching hard among the hills, eager to kill them. God, our Creator, is the Giver of Life. And so all human life ultimately belongs to God; every human being is sacred.

I wanted to tell the soldier, 'All human life is sacred. Your life is sacred. The lives of the young people in the Guerrilla are sacred. The institutional church is not, in itself, sacred. It's the servant of the sacred, the unworthy servant of all human life.

'Besides this, a church service itself, cushioned from human hurt, is not the true, crucified church of Jesus Christ. The church is called to defend and promote human life. Life is sacred; not the institutional church.'

I wanted to tell the soldier that but, on this occasion, judged it wiser to 'retire to my estate and hold my own counsel'.

PABLO
29th June 1987

PABLO IS OLD AND frail, beaten by the years. And because his body can no longer withstand the rigour of working in the maize field, and because there is no such system as social security for the 'campesinos' of El Salvador, Pablo must beg for his daily food. Crouched and leaning on his stick he shuffles slowly to the houses of those who will give him charity. His nearest relatives are themselves too poor to keep him fed.

I used to preach that the poor need justice, not charity. Charity is ineffectual; it's no good mopping up the floor while the tap continues to gush out water. The system needs renewing. I used to speak of getting to the cause of the problem and not being content with treating symptoms. 'Repair the fucking tap; don't mop the floor! Justice, not charity!' was the battle-cry. But the fact is: the system is hopelessly corrupted and sinful. Justice is long-delayed and uncertain. And Pablo's hunger needs to be satisfied here and now.

He comes to our house most mornings and asks for the 'Laying on of hands' and a blessing. Then he goes on his way searching for food. If he's unsuccessful in his quest he'll come and beg charity from us.

Sometimes, Pablo will spend a long time chatting incoherently of past times and past peoples. On one such occasion, as I sat listening, Little Rosa passed by and eavesdropped through the porch's wooden spars.

Later in the day, when I was sitting alone, she returned and said to me, 'Padre, Pablo tells pure lies . . . pure lies.' Raising my eyebrows and smiling I replied, 'Not pure lies, Rosa, only ... imaginative stories.'

Despite his simplicity, Pablo has always struck me as being a sort of 'apocalyptic' figure. Maybe it's the grumpy manner in which he occasionally raises his stick to young kids impeding his passage with their frolics. Maybe it's the unwitting way he voices Sartre's 'We're beings for death' and is overheard talking to Christ about his own death while prostrating himself before the tabernacle. Or maybe he's an apocalyptic figure because, on Judgement Day, Pablo will be sitting beside the Son of Man and telling him how his human dignity was taken away by the unbridled greed of a rich minority.

SUN TREK
July 1987

I FELT FEAR IN the pit of my stomach as the army helicopter's propellers thudded out their menace behind a shield of trees. Machine-gun fire and bombs exploding punctuated the solitude of the muddy road we plod.

Eager to move on unseen and unharmed I cajoled Sab, my visitor from Scotland, to keep going. Unused to the tropical climate, high altitude and uphill climb, he was floundering like a fish out of water. A fitting simile this, because our canisters had run dry an hour before and we had no water.

'Sab, move your fucking legs,' I snapped, exasperated, when he lay on the dirt road and pleaded for respite. Any helicopters preying in the conflict zone are not too careful about whether their targets are military or civilian, as past experience shows, and, if we had been spotted, it's probable that a hail of bullets would have fallen on us.

What seemed like an eternity passed us by, and we proceeded on our way, leaving the sounds of war behind.

Near our destination we met Inocencio, a 'campesino'. He was looking feverish but explained that he had to make the journey through the war-lines in order to visit his sick wife and pay her hospital bills. Typically thin, his eyes watering with high temperature, he told us there were Government soldiers on the road, further on. We shared a few supplies and parted company.

I could see and hear the soldiers grouped together and walking behind the earthen alcove at the side of the road. Not wishing to startle them I put on a clownish, plastic grin under my straw hat and shouted '¡Buenas tardes!' in a tone of pure merriment. Surprise and silence was the reaction and a rifle was pointed at me. Heading for the officer I extended my right hand. The origin of the handshake comes from the Roman custom of showing your sword hand as empty of weapons. It seemed an appropriate gesture under the circumstances.

Fortunately, as I'd been stopped by them at checkpoints on numerous occasions, some of them recognised me. So, after radioing 'Charlie', their chief, on the neighbouring hill, they allowed us to proceed.

We passed downhill through the maize fields and entered the village. In one of the adobe houses I quaffed glasses of water, a glass of lemon drink and a cup of hot milk, seeking to slake the dryness, but only succeeded in causing myself to vomit in the flower-patch outside. The two house-dogs feasted on my stomach contents.

The day before our arrival a soldier from the group we had met walked down through the maize fields to the house we were visiting. He asked the family for 'tortillas', standing in the doorway. Believing him to be one of the Guerrilla searching for food Charlie's group on the opposite hill opened fire. The army bullets crashed through the roof and doorway, cutting holes in the walls of the house. One bullet rebounded from a wall and passed diagonally across a hammock where a young child was fast asleep, narrowly missing him. 'By a miracle of God,' the old woman told us, 'nobody was hurt.' That evening we slumped onto our canvas deck-beds and slept the sleep of innocent babes.

LETTER TO
NIÑA FRANCISCA
10th September 1987

DEAR NIÑA FRANCISCA

A few weeks ago, I took the Bread of the Eucharist to your house and gave you Communion. The pigs, as usual were spanked out of the gate by Paulita, your spinster daughter. The room was dark and Paulita couldn't get a light for the candle stub because the embers in the hive-shaped oven had no life left in them. The room was in darkness as we celebrated Christ, the Light of the World.

Niña Minga tells me that on Sunday Paulita was still trying to get light from the fire embers when you curled up like a child in the womb and passed on through the darkness into the light of heaven.

You suffered a lot of heartbreak in your life, Niña Francisca. You, your husband, and Paulita were exiled from your home in Tremedal. The violence of the death squads was brutal, and your two sons were murdered. You had to leave behind your house and land and live in squalor, going from poverty to misery. You told me the doctor had said the cataracts in your eyes were caused by ceaseless weeping, mourning the loss of your murdered children. This could be so. Tears spring from deep hurt.

Niña Francisca, you've gone home now to heaven, the haven of peace and calm, after the restlessness of stormy waters. You weren't allowed to go home to Tremedal to live out the twilight years of your life. But now no one has the power to stop you going home to God. You're beyond the reach of their violence and death.

I was visiting the other nine communities when you died. Niña Minga tells me you were disappointed at the prospect of burial without a funeral Mass. I'm sorry that's the way it had to be.

Your grieving is over, Niña Francisca, and you've gone home to the Light. Pray a prayer for those of El Salvador who still have to suffer heartache and loss as they journey through life.

Un abrazo,

El Padre.

DEATH'S DOOR
(DANIEL, PART 1 OF 3)
18th November 1987

A GUERRILLA TOLD ME at the bridge one of the civilian prisoners held captive by them in the hills was in deep trouble, but the other one not so deep. Their perplexed relatives and friends feared the worst and asked me, as the priest, to intercede for the accused. So, I wrote thirteen notes to be dispersed to any guerrillas passing by, requesting an opportunity to speak on behalf of the accused.

When I eventually met the zone commander, he told me he had received nine of my notes. There must be a word to describe the neurotic condition of someone who writes thirteen letters saying the same thing to one person. The rebel leader saw the humour and remarked that the 'Padre' was flinging a lot of excrement in his direction.

Tongue in cheek I answered, 'That's right.' And we chuckled.

Then the conversation turned into a serious vein. I put the case to him: 'If they're innocent we want their release. Justice demands this. If they're guilty we ask for mercy. Mercy can take the form of a personal warning to the individuals, or a warning to them in front of the whole community or, as the ultimate chastisement, expulsion from Guerrilla territory, leaving behind their house, lands and community.'

The following afternoon I organised the signing of a petition in the community of the captured requesting their release. More than eighty names were collected before and after Mass. Those unable to write put a cross or a line. And the two copies were sent to the Guerrilla.

At Mass, I preached on the Gospel of the impetuous widow who pestered so that that justice was done for her (Luke 18, 1-8), and as an illustration told a story from the life of Snoopy, the dog:

'One hot day Snoopy placed his water dish under the garden tap. Then he sat down and waited anxiously. Hours passed and still no water would fall.

Of a sudden the skies broke open and rain poured down, filling the water dish to the brim, and Snoopy drank contentedly.

The point of the story is that God answers our prayers with reality. There is no invisible divine hand which turns taps for us.'

Next day I received a message from the FMLN bidding me walk two hours to another community and in the evening the two prisoners would be handed over into my custody.

Before the prisoners were released the rebel representative remarked, 'And over the past few days we've been making some observations on your behaviour.'

'On me?' I asked, wide-eyed, with my forefinger pointed at my chest.

Beto smiled, 'Yes, you . . . Our High Command raised two points. One: your lack of confidence in the FMLN's discernment of justice. And two: creating an agitation of the people. The second point may not always be a bad thing, and we realise you were doing it out of humanitarian motives.'

I admitted the second point and, with regards to the first, told him that I didn't doubt the Guerrilla's sense of justice but, from experience, knew that mercy has not always been an overriding factor in their discernment when it comes to sentencing those guilty of spying.

In the parting speech Daniel was told, 'In other times you would have been executed.' Prior to that, another guerrilla had made it clear to him that his release was a 'novelty'. Be as it may, Daniel and Jorge were delighted at being released alive and well from their twelve-day captivity in the hills and breathed afresh the clear, mountain air with the relish of the freed. They had been granted mercy and had been allowed to walk away from death's door.

THE GRAVE OF A
YOUNG REBEL
17th November 1987

I COULD SENSE THE tension in the atmosphere as I walked into the village. A group of men were standing next to the fence; their faces were solemn and unresponsive. A pall of sadness, perhaps fear, was covering the place.

On enquiry it was revealed that the previous evening a youngster of the Guerrilla had been trapped as he ran from the pursuing soldiers. They were waiting as he ran into their trap like a frightened fox. The hounds tore him apart without mercy. Bullets ripped through his body, disfiguring his face beyond recognition. The people were shocked on seeing this young rebel killed in their village square, lying motionless in blood. A child of sorrows; his face disfigured; bearing the sins of his people.

When the Army retreated the men of Yerba Bueno quickly buried him in a shallow grave and placed splined logs on top to prevent the dogs and pigs from digging and devouring his remains.

I asked if they had prayed at the graveside and the men told me there was no time for that, owing to the threat of further conflict. So, we walked thirty yards and together at the graveside made the sign of the cross, the sign of death and Víctory over death. Then we prayed the Our Father and the words made me feel as if an electric shock were running down my spine.

'Thy Kingdom come.'

May God's reign of justice and human dignity for those who live in dire poverty and hardship come about in our world of today.

'Give us this day our daily bread.'

May those who are deprived of food in our world have food and have it today.

'We forgive those who offend us.'

The prayer of the gentle who will not surrender themselves to hatred of their enemy. Combativeness in war is not hatred.

The Kingdom of God can never be completely identified with any human group (including the Church), but at times essential elements of God's will can be glimpsed in the objectives of certain fallible, human groups.

The young rebel buried in the earth of Viento Bueno was struggling for justice to come about in the lives of his downtrodden people. The restoration of human dignity and the burning desire that the poor might go hungry no more were what he fought and died for.

I have prayed the Lord's Prayer many times in my life, but never before has the prayer moved me so deeply as on that November morning in the hills of El Salvador.

EL IMPERIALISMO
21st November 1987

'JOSÉ MEDARDO AVELAR, ANA Olimpia Avelar, Elisandro Avelar, Sonia Isabet Amaya, Sau Avelar.' It was just a list of names to me, a list spoken by a campesino who asked that they be prayed for in the Eucharist.

'They're all deceased relatives?' I asked, rather clinically.

His eyes moistened with tears and he answered, 'They're my children. They killed them.'

Taken aback by what he was telling me I asked another question, 'Who killed them?'

He almost whispered his reply, 'The Imperialism.'

I questioned no further so as not to cut into unhealed scars. A father's children had been killed by the Army, and he knows that the guns and the bombs and the planes and the helicopters are all sent to El Salvador by the 'Empire' of the United States government. The Empire killed his children. Words on paper don't describe the tears in the eyes of a bereaved father, nor do words convey his soft, sad whisper of 'El Imperialismo'.

CHURCH OF THE POOR
26th November 1987

'HE WAS A WONDERFUL man . . . a wonderful man', said Monseñor Urioste, giving his impression of the assassinated Archbishop Romero. He spoke these words with sincerity and feeling.

The wonderfulness of Óscar Romero was his love and deep concern for the poor, and their love and deep concern for him. He, Prince of the Church, turned to them and they, the defenceless ones plunged as they are in conditions of misery and squalor, turned to him.

Speaking of our work in the parish Monseñor Urioste said, 'If they do not convert you, nobody can.' If the defenceless ones who are being forced to live in abject poverty don't turn your heart and make you more sensitive to the injustice of their living conditions, then your heart is stone and not flesh. The rich live unperturbed, cocooned from the taint of poverty. Wealth and benefits are theirs by birthright. The illness of badly-housed, malnourished children and the sweat of slave-workers who barely eke out an existence is a world apart. 'Communism', they rationalise when any try to better their lot in life.

We set out together, four men and a woman carrying her infant child. For five hours we walked in the heat of the sun along the dusty mountain track. We had arranged to meet Archbishop Rivera y Damas to talk about the possibility of the people returning to their lands and rebuilding their lives. I had delivered the community's letter personally to the Archbishop and had arranged the time of our interview with the secretary. My companions, unknown to me, had confirmed the appointment two weeks after my initial booking. So, we walked with expectations that Archbishop Rivera y Damas would heed the request of these displaced people and speak to the President, seeking immunity from any acts of military reprisal on themselves and their possessions when they return to their lands.

We spent overnight in the parish house, interrupting our journey, and rose at 3.30 a.m. next morning to travel three hours by bus to San Salvador. I marvelled to see them spruced up in a very dignified fashion for their meeting with His Grace. It was to be a big occasion for them. Even Baby Norma wore fine leather bootees. These were clean, but the campesinos' boots still bore the dust of our travels through the hill country. Víctor was limping a bit but made no complaint. One of our company went barefooted – shoes a luxury he never knew.

We arrived at the Archbishop's office and there the secretary told us, 'The Archbishop is indisposed.' One of his Vicars General had gone into his office ahead of us. 'He won't be able to see you before the 15th of December.'

I felt the fire flow through my veins. I said to the secretary, 'This woman here has walked through the hills five hours in the sun and dust carrying her child in order to keep this appointment, and the Archbishop won't allow us five minutes of his time!'

'He's not in,' she lied.

Then she tried to claim we hadn't made any appointment at all. I jerked her memory and also mentioned the campesinos' confirmation of my original booking. She said nothing. We walked away disheartened. My companions were meek and submissive in their humiliation. They're a gentle, patient people.

Outside, a woman from a resettlement help-group who was to accompany us in the interview said: 'Don't worry; that's only the Church. There are other avenues to follow.'

I corrected her, 'That's not the Church. That's the Church's hierarchy. These people here are the Church.' I circled with my finger our rag-tag group.

Later on, recalling happenings, I felt warm tears trickle down my cheeks. Something died within me that day, but something else has come to birth.

THE POOR WITH YOU ALWAYS
11th December 1987

I DON'T FEEL SORRY for the poor. They're worth much more than my lament. I don't want to give them my charity. They're clean, dignified, hard-working people. They're worth much more than pity or charity.

I'm not poor. I have status in society as a Catholic priest. If a poor person is killed it doesn't make headlines in the newspapers. He was anonymous in life and he remains anonymous in death. But if they kill a Catholic priest it makes international headlines; the news is broadcast throughout the world. I'm from the 'first' world, the world of the exploiter. The 'third' world is the world of the exploited. It's a different world. Or maybe it's just the underside of the same world.

By 'first' world standards I live quite frugally, although never suffering malnutrition and never forced to endure bad health through lack of money. Nothing to boast of, yet nothing to be ashamed of. Living quietly beyond the glare of spotlights – without fuss.

The Government soldiers arrived in our village at the beginning of December and the poor queued up for a handful of rice and a handful of frijoles/beans and a piece of clothing sent from the United States. This is the charity of counter-insurgency money used to stave off revolutionary hunger. What father would visit his deprived child in the month of Christmas to give him a sweet, while throughout the year he cares not a whit for his well-being? The sweet is to keep his child from complaining. Such a show of benevolence is bound to impress the watching world!

'Give us this day our daily bread!' cry the hungry children. 'Bread, bread, not bullets!'

We owe them an apology. We must beg pardon of the poor.

DANIEL DASTARDLY
(PART 2 OF 3)
12th December 1987

THE NIGHT CAME CREEPING through the hills, leaving us in semi-darkness. I was standing alone outside the village church when a campesino, carrying his sickle, approached me. I was taken aback. 'Don Daniel, what you doing here?' I gasped. 'The Guerrilla expelled you from their territory; that was their condition for freeing you.'

Weasel-like, eyes bulging, he whispered, 'I'm not going to do what they tell me. Death is sweeter.'

I felt anger come over me. 'It's your life and your death.'

'I've come back out of love for my family,' he reasoned.

'You're no good dead to your family,' I answered. 'Expulsion from the zone lasts till the end of the war. But death is for ever.'

This man made me feel spiritually unclean. I explained to him that I had been trying to promote a possible structure of expulsion as the ultimate chastisement for espionage and he, by his foolhardiness, was destroying any remote possibility of this happening in the future. Others will die as a consequence. He gave the impression of being totally unconcerned about this and he didn't seem to care that, at the moment of speaking to him, another man in the community was being held by the Guerrilla, accused of spying.

Anger inside me was turning into gut-deep revulsion for this cunning, scheming little man whose life had been spared through my efforts. I remembered reading a short poem written by a poet belonging to the Guerrilla. It was entitled 'The Poor Man of the Bourgeoisie'. It read something like:

> Poor man of the bourgeoisie
> You've got no homeland;

You've got no people
You've got no social class;
You've got nothing.
See you, son of a whore,
You can go and screw yourself.

That night I had a dream. I dreamed the palms of both my hands had been bitten by a scorpion. They had become swollen and had turned a gangrenous green. My left hand bore an open wound, stigmatised.

The day of my encounter with Daniel I had been ministering the Sacrament of Reconciliation wherein Christ's pardon and healing are bestowed by the priest laying his hand on each penitent's shoulder and saying words of cleaning (absolution). The palms of a priest's hands are anointed during the ceremony of ordination as a symbol of this healing ministry.

All my personal effort and pleading for clemency the month before had been turned into falsehood. Daniel was, for me, like a scorpion – dangerous and poisonous. My hands had been bitten and gangrened by contact with him. My ministry had been defiled. He had broken a bond of honour and abused the mercy shown him. He is a poor man of the bourgeoisie and he can go and screw himself.

CHRISTMAS TEARS
29th December 1987

THE FESTIVE SEASON IS being celebrated worldwide. It is four o'clock in the afternoon and I walk towards the church in Barrio San Marcos, San Salvador. Up the hill; past the vendors' stalls which strew the pavements; past the group of soldiers from the nearby barracks, and round the corner. There I see a small group of people standing outside the town hall, staring silently at a man lying with his right knee bent upwards. 'Must be drunk,' I think. Then I see the dark red blood splattered over his face and side, forming a pool on the cement.

'What's the matter with him?' I ask a youngster.

'He's dead. They killed him. They left two bodies, but they took one away again,' he answers.

'Who killed the two men, then?'

'I don't know,' he answers, his gaze not meeting mine.

A fly settles on the victim's left shoulder. 'The Death Squad.' A woman's voice from the group breaks the silence.

I feel helpless inside. I want to do something to help this motionless, blood-splashed victim, but he is beyond human help. Maybe I should say a prayer with the people who are standing next to the corpse but, numbed, I walk on to speak with the Italian parish priest in the church building.

'Yes, there were two of them. Put there at mid-day . . . It's a great tragedy. They are not from here; their identity papers were found on them . . . you know, Father, I've just come from anointing a dying man in his house. He was comforted by the sacraments and surrounded by his loved ones. The death of these men is very different.'

The kindly priest ushers me into the back rooms to inspect the structural damage caused by last year's earthquake and to show off his rebuilding programme. We engage in polite conversation for a while and then I take leave of him.

Today, in San Salvador, Christ was crucified and killed.

1988

CHILD OF EPIPHANY
5th January 1988

ON THE EVE OF the Epiphany, in a remote hill country village, I walked to a house in order to pay my respects to Marta Gladis. She was a year old when she died. This was to have been the day of her baptism. As I walked, I felt empty inside. I had no token of love to offer this child, and if I had, the love token would have been myrrh, the burial nard for the dead.

Shyly I approached the first house. The carpenter was joining together pieces of wood for the coffin. 'We're made for suffering in this world,' he mused. The family would have to carry their child's remains for two and a half hours, walking in the heat of the sun, before reaching the burial plot. A long, hard journey of sadness. This was to have been the day of her baptism, but she had died the previous night at 10 o'clock, suffering from vomiting and diarrhoea, a sickness common to malnourished children. It was to be the day of her funeral.

Those who study theology often tell us that baptism means being given over to death in order to break through into new life. It is participation in Christ's death in order to participate in his Resurrection from death. The child's parents told me that they had 'poured the water' on the little one before she had died. She had been given over to death through the sacrament of baptism in the silent, confident hope of passing into an unknown, new life. She was now 'an angel of God', as the simple faith of the campesinos would have it.

I entered the room where Marta Gladis lay. She seemed like a sleeping doll, her features waxened by death. She was dressed in a white, 'bridal' robe and surrounded with freshly-plucked wild flowers. Lit candles shed light on her remains, breaking down the darkness.

During the Lord's Prayer her mother stifled a sob. 'Give us this day our daily bread.' For lack of daily bread their child had died. 'Deliver us from evil.' And it is evil that this should happen.

'Epiphany' is 'manifestation of God'. The crucified God has been revealed in the death of Marta Gladis.

THE SHADOW OF REALITY
7th January 1988

THE TROOPS WERE FILING down through the village when
the Guerrilla opened fire on them from a nearby hill. Hearing
the heavy rattle of machine-gun bullets, we moved for cover into
the front room of the house, trying to keep ourselves outside the
parameters of the wooden shutters for fear of any stray bullets.

The soldiers crouched next to the house and returned fire.
The loud thud of bullets signalled danger and we huddled nervously
inside. Twelve-year-old Sandra began to cry, hysterically letting
out what sounded to me like nervous laughter. This blended with
the bullets' thudding. Then she flung herself under the bed. Even
her golden Labrador looked sad and disorientated. Sandra's mum
moved her lips in prayer, sitting on the bed above her daughter.
Following her good example, I tried to pray in my mind the
second part of the Ave Maria:

'Holy Mary, Mother of God, pray for us sinners now, and at
the hour of our death.'

The thought crossed my mind. 'That's a prayer I don't pray
very often.'

The bullets continued to rattle, and I felt a bit fidgety, an
added factor to my agitation being the effect of two cups of coffee
I had drunk that morning.

After about twenty minutes, silence fell, and the troops
moved out. I passed to the toilet without disgracing myself, then
joined the others in the dusty street.

On the hill, about five hundred yards distance, smoke was
belching upwards; a fire had been caused by the soldiers' bazooka
bombs, and some of the villagers were seen to be hurrying in
that direction, hoping to extinguish the flames and save their
crop of 'maicito' (maize) from further damage.

Meanwhile small boys searched in the dust for empty bullet-
shells (of which there were plenty). These they stuffed into their

pockets to use as whistles. In Spain, the Spanish people have a tradition wherein the three kings gift toys to the children on the Feast of the Epiphany, 6th of January. Empty cartridges were to be the precious toys of these grubby, shoeless children.

I watched them. Bubbling with excitement they began to re-enact the whole drama, stuttering out the sounds of guns and shaking their fists and make-believe machine-guns towards the hills. 'Shadows cast by the true'. Their fantasy world was shadowing grim reality. Some day in the future, grim reality will probably overshadow their fantasy world.

IN REMEMBRANCE
15th January 1988

JOSÉ ROBERTO FOUND IT amusing that a priest should be walking through the village carrying a tray of eggs. Flip-flopping down the slope in my plastic sandals, I did not stop to greet this grinning Guerrilla and his companions, partly because of the likelihood that an army spy network operates in the main village of our parish, and partly a feeling of acute embarrassment at being caught doing the shopping. I mean, John Wayne would not be caught doing the messages; it taints the macho image somewhat.

José Roberto was his war-name. He picked as his pseudonym the names of his two children because he loved them and wanted them to live in a better, more just homeland. For this he was prepared to sacrifice his life.

'My father is very rich. Two cars. Big house. I was a student at the university and had a promising career ahead of me. One day I lay on my bed, looked at the ceiling and said to myself: "It's not right. People in El Salvador are living and dying in squalor, and here am I, comfortable, in high living."'

So, he joined the Guerrilla.

I remember over a year ago we sat in a village community in the hills to the north. As the candle burned in the middle of the porch, we shared oranges and ideas. The conversation was vibrant. I was speaking about the sinfulness of the Church, and he spoke about the wrongs committed by the Guerrilla in the early years. 'The people never forget,' José Roberto told me. 'Nowadays the Guerrilla treat the civilian population with respect, but in the early part of the war it was not always so. And the people never forget.'

I reflected, 'Often we've betrayed Christ. Often we've twisted his liberating message to suit our own convenience.'

'We laugh at the Russian image of Communism – so sober, so joyless. Our revolution is filled with happiness. It's different,' he explained to me. 'Sometimes when I'm washing myself in a river, I say my name over and over again, just to remind myself who I really am.'

The conversation penetrated into the night. We had been chatting for five hours and more. So, wearied and contented, we called it a day.

At 6.45pm on Sunday the 13th of December 1987, a burst of gunfire pierced the night. Next day I left the main village to visit the other villages further north, not knowing what had happened. I imagined the Guerrilla to have ambushed soldiers outside the village.

Before setting off, I overheard a soldier stationed in our porch ask, 'Only one dead?'

'Yes, only one,' the other replied.

I did not know who the dead person was. It was almost a month later I discovered that in the darkness of that night the soldiers had riddled 'with about twenty-five bullets' the body of José Roberto. Later, they had stolen his watch from his wrist. They had also taken a bag of money he was carrying to buy food, also his folder of information. And, following the Salvadorean Army's barbaric habit, they had cut off the left ear of the slain guerrilla in order to take it back to barracks as a trophy.

The villagers had to leave José Roberto's corpse throughout the night, lying beneath the mango tree where he had fallen. The following morning, they found that the pigs and dogs had eaten away a large part of his flesh. His right leg had been wrenched apart; the dogs were devouring it at the other side of the wire fence. 'The dogs were full,' a woman told me.

Today, thirty-three days later, I went to pray the Lord's Prayer at José Roberto's grave. I noticed his congealed blood splattered on the bushes and the mango tree, which had also been heavily chipped by the bullets. It was also noticeable that Don Luís had not dug the grave deeply enough, and flies and ants covered the place where José Roberto was laid to rest.

After praying, we set about collecting stones and placed them on the grave. I shooed away a piglet. Eventually, we piled a mound of stones over the remains. Stone symbolizes the eternal. It is appropriate that there be a sign of the undying near the shredded remains of José Roberto. Truth will never be silenced. This man's love for his suffering people can never die.

A young lad, seeing me and the others putting stones on top of the grave laughed and said flippantly, 'He's not going to come out of there, Padre.'

I looked into the youngster's eyes and replied, 'No, but there will be a resurrection. He will rise.'

The smile disappeared, and the youngster fell into silence.

HEAVEN'S WISDOM
3rd February 1988

CÉSAR IS AN EIGHT-year-old mongol child, a 'moon baby' who will always have a child's understanding of the world even when he is older and enters adulthood.

On seeing me arriving in the village where he lives, he rushes off and tells his Gran. He grunts and makes the sign of the cross from forehead, to shoulders, to tummy. It makes me feel privileged to be associated with the sign of Christ's cross, even if made askew.

Sometimes when I tire of talking Spanish, I relax and blether to César in English, my mother tongue. And I feel he understands me better than anybody. Well, by all accounts, he definitely understands me when we munch Mr Lido's Cream Biscuits together, and he glugs down water from my aluminium container.

César sees things as if he is seeing them for the very first time. He takes me by the hand and leads me into an abandoned house inhabited now by straying pigs. Once inside, he looks up to the wooden rafters and orange clay tiles and points out the white pigeons, making a squeaking noise. He remains transfixed in wonderment. I then mimic the birds too and make a sort of flapping motion with my arms. We both agree: God's creation is wonderful.

A pig makes heavy weather of copulating with a sow. Despite repeated attempts the pig fails to reach its target, being by far too small for his high-hinded sow. Gargoyle-like, César ogles, points his finger, and emits a syllable of amusement. He tugs my sleeve and I avert my gaze to the skies, blushing with embarrassment.

At Communion time, during our liturgical celebration, César approaches the altar. Leaning over he stares at the Bread of the Eucharist and signals to me that he wants to eat too. He is persistent, because this is the third occasion which he has done this. His beady eyes appeal: 'We munched biscuits together, why not this?' But, feeling inhibited, I refuse him the Bread of the Eucharist.

During the baptisms which follow Mass he crawls under my alb as I stand addressing the people. His head bulges out from under the white vestment, making me appear to be suffering from a swollen knee cap. César, our nomadic camper, chuckles aloud. This is hilarious. Psalm 84 sums it all up, 'How lovely are thy tents, Lord, God of Hosts.'

Don Mario, César's father, says, 'Nature has denied César the wisdom of this earth, but he has been given in its stead the wisdom of heaven.'

I agree.

PARADISE OF THE POOR
4th March 1988

IT WAS A JOURNEY into the unknown. El Higueral had been abandoned for seven years. A number of its villagers, many of them old people or children, were killed by the invasion of the Government soldiers on the 14th of February 1981.

Beto, the young man from the neighbouring village of El Barrancón, told me how his mother had been stripped, tied to a bed, gang-raped and killed by the death-squad. He said, 'We found the two cartridges of their bullets beside her head. Her body was eaten away by worms . . . but the vultures didn't get at her remains because they killed her in the house.'

We walked by the riverside path which would veer off uphill towards El Higueral, situated amongst a clump of trees. 'When they killed Monseñor Romero I wept tears,' he continued, 'but I didn't cry when they killed my mother.' Perhaps it happens that emotions die, and tears dry up when someone is shocked beyond the limits of human capacity.

It was an eerie experience entering the womb which had once held the life of a people. This evening it was more like a tomb of dilapidated houses and bitter memories of death. The voices of the people echoed in the distance and as we approached, they came to meet us, smiles of welcome on their faces. They were thrilled to receive Archbishop O'Brien as he came into their midst, riding a mule.

That evening the Archbishop presided at the celebration of the Eucharist. We stacked sacks of corn to serve as the altar, and in the darkness of the night we prayed for the dead of El Higueral and for those who were now intent on bringing new life to the village.

The moon shone full and the stars sparkled as we bedded down on Mother Earth. One person told the Archbishop, 'This is the Paradise of the Poor!' Perhaps he was making a pun on the army garrison which is named 'Paradise', verbally playing on the contrast. Or perhaps a pun was unintentional. But, be as it may, the Exodus people had planted a seed of hope and were set on bringing new life to El Higueral.

ADIÓS, DON PABLO
18th March 1988

LA NIÑA LAURA, PABLO'S old, barefooted sister came to see me yesterday. Restraining tears, she said, 'Pablo called for you four times, Padrecito. He wanted to say "Goodbye". But you weren't here, and he wouldn't believe me. He told me he had seen you going to the shop the day before, but how could he? He was nearly blind as well as deaf, and mentally wandering.'

I felt sad at not having been present to bid him farewell. The surly Pablo reminded me of the old Scotsman who, on his death-bed, was asked if he wanted more prayers and scripture readings. He was tired and answered, 'Ah theekit ma hoose when the weather wiz warm'. Pablo had made sure no tiles had become loosened from his house long before the rains fell. His salvation did not depend on the oils of a church sacrament. However, I would have liked to have been present, just to say goodbye.

Niña Laura told how, before Pablo died, he had got her to dress him with the clothes he had been gifted. He named each item of clothing and the person who had given him it. He put on the white shirt his niece's son had gifted him, the trousers given him by Blanca, his niece. And so on. Then, knowing he was going on his last journey, he sent for flowers, and an old woman at the top of the street gifted him flowers.

Pablo always kept a peso-note in his shirt pocket to pay for the nails of his coffin. He never had the money with which to buy the whole coffin. But Jesus, too, occupied a borrowed tomb after his crucifixion. The disgrace of this is not in the poor person, but in the social situation which permits and fosters such poverty. As it happened, after his death, a couple of men in the village bought Pablo his coffin.

Death was a release. A few months before he died I went to visit him. His niece, Blanca, met me at the door. She looked and sounded at the end of her tether. 'I don't know what to do with him, Padrecito. He went off to see you this morning. His mind has gone a bit loco and now he's down the embankment.' In his last months, owing to a fall, Pablo could not walk. He used to pull himself from place to place in a seated position.

I looked down the embankment and there he was, sitting on the rubbish dump, a modern-day suffering Job, planted on his dung-heap. I got help; a young lad and me lifted him to the street. It was difficult to suppress the humorous side of the situation. The image of Steptoe, the rag-and-bone merchant of television, with his toothless grin, crossed my mind's eye. Later in the day I asked myself when Pablo was going to make that longer journey beyond this life's rubbish dump.

On Saturday, 5th of March 1988, old Pablo passed on to the Judgement Seat of God, but not to stand before it and be judged. Not he. Pablo and all the poor will be seated as our judges on the Last Day. Jesus promises that it will be so: 'I was hungry and you gave me no food; I was thirsty and you never quenched my thirst; I was an outcast and you didn't receive me into your house; I had no clothing and you didn't clothe me; I was sick and imprisoned and you didn't come to visit me' (Mt. 25, 42-43). And on that day we will not be able to avoid the consequences of having lived in the presence of God's Poor.

THE LIFE OF THE TREES
23rd March 1988

I FELT LIKE I had been ordered to take a decisive, last-minute spot-kick in a World Cup Final while, with bated breath, the crowds looked on. Jesus must have experienced this same uneasy sensation when his inquirers asked, 'Master, what do you think?' (Mark 12, 14.)

Don Ángel spoke up, 'The lads of the Guerrilla held a public meeting and have forbidden us to fell any more trees in the area. They're preventing us from working. We desperately need the money from timbering to support our wives and families. What do you advise us to do?'

That dreaded question had been publicly levelled at me. I stood before the people having celebrated the Eucharist with them, still wearing the white alb and stole. I looked at them. They waited for my reply.

I drew a breath. 'Eighteen months ago, Don Toño, an old man, spoke to me of his fear for the future. The people tell me he has healing in his hands. I, personally, regard him as a seer. He envisages a threat posed by this present generation, a threat which will deprive future generations of the earth's resources. The fear he expressed was to do with the death of the wood industry in these parts. Owing to the war economy of El Salvador, the poor people are struggling to make ends meet and, in desperation, they are cutting down and selling as much wood as they can. Yet no sapling trees are being sown to replace them. Don Toño, this wise old man, also pointed out the destruction of the woodland caused by mortars or incendiary bombs dropped from the war planes, and the burning done during military operations. The signs of pending death for the wood industry of El Salvador scar the land. Ash and smoke and creeping flame cover what used to be beautiful hillside. Our water resources are drying up. Future generations are going to suffer the consequences of our actions.

'I'm a priest. I'm not a married man with a family to support. I don't feel the hardship and sacrifice the way you do. I may be wrong in what I'm saying, but I feel that our present generation needs to make a sacrifice for the sake of our children's children.

'The prohibition measures imposed by the Guerrilla are hard, but they're not unjustified. They reflect the concern of old Don Toño. Things are bad here, but in the city the poor can't even find firewood, and they have no land to till and grow crops.

'You, the people, wanted me to speak to the Guerrilla last month, and I did so. They advise that for three consecutive months you plant a hundred new trees and, at the end of this period, send a representative to talk to them about the problem. I see this as fair enough. They're not closing doors on the problem. It's a means of conservation to balance the destruction which is taking place. But let's not just concentrate on the symptoms. The real root of this disease is the war and its causes. If there comes about a just, dignified, true and lasting peace to El Salvador this problem and others like it will disappear.'

The Community's spokesman spoke again, 'That's fine. We just wanted your counsel on the subject.' I returned, 'No counsel can cure hunger.'

A CHILD'S PRAYER
29th April 1988

LATE IN THE EVENING I washed the dirt from where the thorn had pierced her bare foot. 'It's sore,' the child whined. Little María del Carmen watched attentively as I wiped the bit of soap over her wound, and slowly the dirt dissolved and disappeared. Then I put on the disinfectant cream and taped a gauze pad over the hurt. With her big, brown, pleading eyes she resembled a baby doe. '¡Gracias!' she shouted and ran off.

The following day, I was sitting on a tree which, seven years ago, had been struck down by a mortar bomb. María del Carmen came up to me and held out a single red flower. 'Padre,' she said. I took the flower from her hand and, without a word more, she turned and walked away.

It was a small gesture, perhaps very insignificant in the course of world events. But it meant a lot to me. It seemed to instil new life in a place which had suffered painful death. It was a symbol of childlike simplicity during a very complicated war. It was innocence replacing violence. A red flower in the tender hand of a child had made stark opposition to a rifle in the calloused hands of a soldier. It was a child's prayer for the future of El Salvador.

CHILD'S PLAY
11th October 1988, Los Llanitos

SYLVIA IS THREE YEARS old and still a trifle unsteady walking. She gurgles with excitement as her little bare feet pitter-patter on the grass, trying to grasp the empty medicine bottle before her older brother, Chus. Chus bounces the bottle down the embankment, counting the rebounds it makes, and runs to reach it before Sylvia. He always gets there first.

Sylvia wearies and sits down to rest on the step, beside me. Awed by my key-ring she jingles the keys and blurts out a syllable and looks up at me.

'Young lady, thou shalt not covet thy neighbour's goods,' I muse with a smile. Her nose is dripping catarrh and I wipe it clean with a tissue. This I do out of no altruistic motive; I got the feeling shy Sylvia was going to snuggle her face into my shoulder. No show of affection, you understand, just the sheer pragmatic need of a good nose-clean.

Chus has found a broken plastic lid and he flings it through the air. 'Look, a flying saucer! . . . Oh crumbs, it's got stuck.'

I step forward, a giant in the land of the elves, and shake the UFO from the tree.

Loud bombing sounds in the distance, coming from the hill called 'The Little Wheatfield' ('El Trigalito'), although no wheat is now grown in that area.

'Phew, those are big bomb bangs, eh?' Chus remarks.

'Not half,' I agree.

A few moments later Chus's little brother, Juan, is set to stick a dessert spoon into a furry caterpillar which is slowly creeping along the tin church door. I rescue the insect and, in procession with the children, gently carry it to a place of safety, putting it on a high branch of a tree.

I look at the children. 'You see this little caterpillar? Someday it will shed its furry coat and turn into a butterfly, and it will have freedom, and it will be able to fly far, far away.'

HALLOWEEN
31st October 1988

I FELT UNEASY AND couldn't sleep. Normally, I sleep very
soundly, but tonight I was restless. Maybe it was something to
do with witches cackling, black cats' green eyes staring, and
bright stars in the sky shining. Whatever the reason I got out
of bed, went to the kitchen, drank a coke, ate a banana and
two biscuits and killed a cockroach with the fly-swatter. Then
I went to the toilet and spotted a black scorpion on the wall.
I crushed it with a plastic basin. I checked that the porch light
was still on as I passed on my way to bed again.

Still sleep wouldn't overtake me. I tossed and turned to
and fro until two o'clock in the morning when I heard people
speaking in the porch. I thought it was the soldiers. A few nights
ago, they had asked me to put out the light-bulb of the outer
porch so that they could sleep there. I made up a story about the
Bishop forbidding us to do this at night-time, the light being a
sign of our availability and presence to the people and all that.
They had accepted my pious lie, being more gullible than I gave
them credit for.

Suddenly, there was a loud explosion outside and the sheet
light in my bedroom burst into a thousand pieces and landed on
the floor. The house shook as the air vibrated. The force raised
me into the air and also blew the wooden bars off the window-
shutters. Quickly, I put my clothes on and went into our inner
courtyard. My first thought was that the soldiers had planted a
bomb in the porch. Then it occurred to me that there are easier
ways of extinguishing a light bulb. My mind turned to the bats
which had been swooping across the rafters of our house. I felt
sure the explosion would have at least knocked the excrement
out of them. Then another explosion occurred, and I realised
that the Guerrilla had just bombed away the Government
Registrar Office and the village's telephone exchange. The

Registrar's office had been newly painted with the intention of moving village records back into it. At the present they're kept in a village adjacent to the army barracks. The telephone exchange had a lousy line anyway.

From the inner courtyard I could see orange flames darting into the night air, licking a wisp of smoke. The fire crackled, devouring timber. I went to the front of the house and from the porch watched the inferno blaze. Then slowly I went indoors, cleaned up the broken glass from the floor, cleared the debris off my bed and fell asleep.

Next morning at six o'clock, I saw two glum, rather sheepish-looking soldiers standing in the porch. I bade them a good day and got a half-hearted response. I imagined a proud father pushing a pram home only to discover that somehow, somewhere on the way, he had lost the baby.

That morning Lito came to me drunk asking counsel, and María, an old woman who was left mentally retarded and dumb late in life as a result of illness, came weeping, frightened by the explosion. She pointed to a small statue of Our Lady of Fatima in our hallway so, to console her and to encourage my iconoclastic penchant, I gifted María the image and shuffled her towards the door. Her face beamed happiness.

Then to crown it all, as María was leaving, I noticed a woman shouting at an army officer. I put on my shoes and went to see what the commotion was about. The Military had captured three people. Two young men were sitting on the ground held prisoner, and the screaming woman made it three. I got my straw hat and went with them, trekking the hot, dusty road in the middle of a military escort. We reached San Rafael and a lorry took us to Paraíso barracks. There the two men had their thumbs tied behind their backs with shoelaces. They entered and I had to wait an hour at the main gate before talking my way towards permission to go to the inner gate. There a lieutenant checked that the prisoners were there (I knew that already) and asked me to return in forty-eight hours. I told him I'd be back the following day.

Maybe the two things which most poignantly symbolize the atmosphere of this day are: the heavy chunk of metal found in our garden (it flew over our roof from forty yards away); and the ripped playing card among the rubble. The card showed the seven of spades. Seven is the number of Lady Luck. Spades is the sign of death. Both luck and death loomed over us today.

HERE COMES THE SUN
31st December 1988

I SAT ON THE steps of the church in the cold morning light, feeling a bit down in the dumps owing to recent happenings. The day before I had arrived in San Fernando Antiguo to celebrate the feast of Corpus Christi with Eucharist, procession and song through the streets. The feast-day arrangements had been made previously with the community and agreed upon. Unknown to me, Machiavellian machinations had been going on behind the scenes in order to alter these arrangements. The protagonist of these alterations was Emilio, a wealthy cattle baron who, for years, had held the title of 'Mayordomo', 'Head Steward of the Church', whose function is to pay the priest for feasts by making door-to-door collections. We don't accept payment for celebrating the people's feast day, only whatever falls in the collection plate at Mass. We would like to make this man's function defunct. He very rarely attends church and there is an unconfirmed suspicion that he may be in receipt of money through a corruption racket with the local government. The local Mayor (who is forced to live outside the Guerrilla-controlled zone) charges the people an additional twenty-five centavos tax each time they pay their water bill. The stamp has the words 'patron feast' printed on it.

I had made feast-day arrangements with Mario, a shy, diminutive, deaf Celebrator of the Word, without consulting Big Emilio, and he was annoyed. On arriving in the village, I had harsh words with him, using strong body-language gestures such as irately turning my back on him. I would have preferred a full-blown confrontation to clear the air but, to put it in metaphor, he shielded himself well behind the Celebrator of the Word and wouldn't come out of his corner into the middle of the ring. However, later, I blew out like an erupted volcano at the Celebrator of the Word, which I regret now because he had been manipulated by Emilio. A weed should be pulled at the roots, not at the stem. The upshot of all this commotion was that no feast was celebrated in San Fernando Antiguo and I moved on, under a dark cloud, to the neighbouring village.

The morning after, a sad song played inside me. I sat in the chill of the early day, desolate, on the church steps. Then came a beautiful experience of healing, a trumpet blast of angels, a soothing of my troubled soul. Six-year-old Gloria came paddling bare-footed through the dust towards me. She carried a sauce bottle filled with a black, watery substance and two bits of stale bread. Her smile beamed warmth and the sun began to rise over the distant hills.

'Hello, Padre. My mum has sent you coffee.'

She sat down and we shared the hot coffee. She giggled when I told her I thought she was bringing me beer. 'We don't buy beer,' she said. I was going to say, 'Neither do I,' but thought it better not to tell lies to the children.

Then young Eladio, about fourteen years of age, arrived carrying a small tin pitcher of hot coffee. He as the second bearer of gifts within a five-minute spell. These small signs of affection make you feel good inside. I felt as if I had been gifted the treasures of the Magi. The stone steps turned into a king's throne. I was being healed by the Poor. They were letting me know I had worth and was appreciated by them. The song of sadness drifted away and a melody of the Beatles played in my head, 'Here comes the sun. Here comes the sun. It's alright.'

1989

BIRTHDAY CRACKERS
20th January 1989

SITTING ON A ROCK I looked down below and admired the beauty of the Salvadorean hills. It was calm after the previous night's bombing. The Air Force planes had dropped Bengali lights and sprayed blood-red bullets through the blackness towards the solid mass of hills and trees. Today provided a sheer contrast. I savoured the calm and felt grateful to God for the thirty-three years of life I had enjoyed to this day. I had been given a span of time, a quality of living which had been denied many young people of El Salvador. They had died before their time, cut off in the bloom of their youth, blooded by a rifle in their hands. To compose the symphony of life, said St Augustine, God makes use of short, broken notes and long, whole notes. Overall there is musical diversity and ordered unity.

The oranges Don Esteban had gifted me tasted sweet. I spat out the remaining pips, picked up my string bag and climbed on up the path. Suddenly, coming towards me I spotted the first in a long line of Government soldiers. Hell's bells, I thought, and greeted the first one with a smile, judging a grin to be a bit too emphatic under the circumstances. By a quirk of chance, he recognised me as the priest. After a brief exchange of words, I continued, half-hypnotised by the incessant procession of green blobs that skirted past me. In total, they stopped and questioned me eight times along the way at various points. On the third occasion an aggressive soldier ordered me to drop my bag. I had introduced myself as the priest, but this only fuelled him to search through my things more thoroughly.

'How little confidence the Armed Forces have in the Church,' I lamented, trying to produce compunction.

His lips formed an evil, hard curve. 'Yes,' he answered. An officer of unknown rank came and sat beside the place where we stood, his rifle placed potently between his legs. 'The Armed Forces are causing you a lot of bother, aren't they?'

'Certainly are,' I answered. This wasn't the reply he expected.

'Are these medicines yours?' asked the soldier with the sadistic smile, holding up a small plastic bag with a dozen sticking plasters inside. I wondered if he really thought I was going to treat more than six thousand guerrillas with a dozen sticking plasters. I concluded he must be either suffering from an over-active imagination or shell-shock.

'They're for my blisters.'

Then he poked his nose into a copy of standard prayers I had jotted down in Spanish.

'Those are prayers . . . "Blessed be God. Blessed be his holy name".'

The official brandishing the phallic symbol butted in. 'Who are you to come to our country and shout at Salvadoreans?'

'I'm not shouting.'

'You are shouting.'

'I'm not shouting,' I repeated. The thought crossed my mind: I'm talking to someone whom only his mother could love.

'Why are there so many foreigners going about loose in those parts?' he retorted.

'I'm not going about loose. I am going to celebrate Mass.' His mother has a lot to answer for, I thought.

'Do you know Octavio Cruz?'

'I know him. He's a priest in a different diocese.'

'He's giving money to the Guerrilla. Did you know that the Guerrilla is basically funded by International Aid?'

I thought of the millions of dollars of weaponry that the United States government continues injecting into the Salvadorean Army in order that they kill the poor. 'The Pastoral Programme for Social Aid of the San Salvador Archdiocese,' I commented, 'helps repopulations; it doesn't fund the Guerrilla.'

'That's a pretext,' said he. 'The repopulations consist of Guerrilla people, all of them. Do you know about line six of the Guerrilla project? It's to spread their people throughout the country.'

'I don't know about that. All I know is that there's a civilian population in the repopulations.'

He looked at me, annoyed. 'What God do you believe in?' he persisted. 'I pray that you change.'

'We all need conversion,' I told him.

'I pray that you change your tone.' He stood up, made a disparaging accusation that the Archbishop of San Salvador and his Auxiliary Bishop were collaborators of the Guerrilla, shook my hand tightly and remarked, 'We'll see each other in Sweden.' Away he went.

He got my nationality wrong, but I didn't correct him. Some people are incorrigible.

THE CROSS
9th February 1989

'SOLDIERS,' WHISPERED NIÑA HILDA. The atmosphere
in the corrugated-tin hut turned tense. All of a sudden, fifteen
yards from us, gunfire broke out, puncturing the evening air.
The soldier with the machine-gun maintained concentrated fire
into the trees. We crouched, lying on the dirt floor, vulnerable,
realising that a spray of bullets could pass easily through the thin
tin. Jorge shielded his youngest child; Hilda another. I huddled
over little Chavelita. My mind was numbed.

'Are you ticklish?' I asked Chavelita, speaking against the
thudding noise of bullets.

She looked at me, wide-eyed, without saying a word,
and started to giggle. There is nothing so contradictory and
anomalous in life as looking at a little girl's laughing face while
outside bullets fly, menacing death.

Call it Divine Providence or call it Lady Luck, the firing
ceased, and we picked ourselves off the ground, unscathed. El
Higueral has not always been so fortunate.

Six months ago, on the evening of the third of August
1988, soldiers arrived there unexpectedly and fired with their
rifles between the tin huts, putting to flight a few guerrillas
who had been taking refuge from the torrential rain. A soldier
stalked towards the doorway of one hut and indiscriminately
fired inside. 'Pull out the corpses of those two terrorists inside!'
he shouted at another soldier.

'They're not guerrillas,' answered the second soldier,
discovering the truth of what had happened. 'They're two old
people.'

Pedro Caballero was within a decade of being a hundred
years old. He was blind, and one of his hands had been amputated
owing to an accident at work some years ago. Blood now gushed
from a bullet wound in his head as he lay dead. The old man

had been eating his supper. His spinster daughter, Nicolasa, was grinding corn. The bullets struck them dead. The blood of the innocent spilled over the earthen floor.

Six months later, the people erected a cross of wood to mark the place where Don Pedro and Niña Nicolasa were killed. The cross was an instrument of execution; it is also a Christian symbol which proclaims the defeat of death. The Oppressor crucifies the Innocent; the Poor Ones of history are scorned and smitten by the Powerful. But the weak will struggle through darkness into light. The Poor will, one day, inherit the earth.

THE SUBVERSION OF THE GOSPEL
17th March 1989

TIRED AFTER THE FOUR-HOUR climb along the mountain track, I walked alone through the streets of Dulce Nombre, certain in the knowledge that soldiers were going to detain and question me. In fact, of the three occasions, the first was the most revealing. It showed, in typical fashion, the suspicion and mistrust that the Armed Forces harbour towards any honest appraisal and application of the Gospel values to the Salvadorean situation. The Gospel in the hands of a peasant who understands the full implications of its message impels him or her to bring about radical individual change and radical change within the whole sinful structure of society.

The soldier searched through my string bag and pulled out Pope John Paul II's Lenten Letter. He eyed it suspiciously. Then he showed off a little that he could read: '. . . to share with a sense of solidarity your possessions.'

Then he came to a really subversive bit of the booklet. I had scribbled in the margin a list of the necessities of the Poor which need to be satisfied: Food, water, consolation, protection, health and freedom. He questioned me. 'This list . . . What does it mean?'

I stood beside him and pointed to the text. 'It's from Matthew's Gospel. Food corresponds to "I was hungry, and you fed me".' I thought, You, the Armed Forces, habitually impede the passage of food supplies to the centres of repopulation, accusing the people of sharing their food with the Guerrilla. '"I was thirsty, and you gave me a drink." Water.' I thought, You, the Armed Forces, dropped your excrement in the water tank belonging to the people who repopulated in Guarjila. '"I was a stranger and you received me into your home." Consolation.' I thought, You, the Armed Forces, consider all strangers to be guerrillas, especially if they are foreigners working with the Poor in the countryside. '"I was naked, and you clothed me." Protection.' I thought, You, the Armed Forces, have tortured, raped and killed the poor and defenceless. ' "I was sick, and you went to visit me." Health.' I thought, You, the Armed Forces, try to prevent the people from having medical supplies, claiming they are used to tend the Guerrilla wounded. '"I was in prison and you came to see me". Freedom.' I thought, You, the Armed Forces, imprison in Mariona those who sympathise with the Revolution.

The word 'subversion' means 'to turn something from underneath'. It means root-deep change in society brought about by the organisation and movement of the Poor, the toppling of repressive structures, the heralding in of a new order of justice and more equal sharing. The Gospel of Christ embodies these human, social values, because it is first and foremost the Gospel of the Poor, and because to them (and perhaps exclusively to them) belongs the Kingdom of God.

EASTER BELLS
22nd March 1989

'An unbelievably sweet yearning
Drove me to roam through wood and lea
Crying, and as my eyes were burning,
I felt a new world grow in me.'

Faust

I EXAMINED THE JUMBLE of emotions experienced by me as I encountered the military checkpoints after walking through the hills of Guerrilla territory into army-controlled territory. I was embarrassed at being stopped by the soldiers while civilians in Dulce Nombre stared on. I was humiliated by their questioning and didn't like having to explain myself to them like a caught-out schoolboy. I was indignant at them pulling the Pope's Lenten Letter from my string bag and peering through it suspiciously as if it were revolutionary propaganda. I felt vulnerable and afraid because I know they have power over me to the point of death. Last month (on the 13th of February) this same battalion of Atlacatl murdered captured prisoners. They raped three female guerrilla health workers (one of them when she was dead) and murdered seven more guerrilla wounded and maimed. They prised out their eyes and cut off their ears; a customary barbaric ritual of theirs. Recalling this, I felt a strange mixture of fear and anger, and wondered if any of these soldiers in front of me had participated in the savagery.

I had to produce my identity documents for them on three occasions along the way. On the third, tedious occasion, in San Rafael, a soldier doubted that the fingerprints on two documents were mine. I would have laughed if I weren't feeling anger surging up from within. In summary, a mixed bag of emotions (embarrassment, humiliation, indignation, fear and stifled anger) was consciously experienced by me on these three encounters.

On the third occasion two old ladies came forward to confirm to the soldiers what I had already told them; that I was the priest of San Francisco. At this point they ordered me to come with them to speak to their chief. I asked, 'Am I arrested? Yes or no.'

'No,' he replied.

'Well, if I were arrested, I'd have to go with you but, being as I'm not arrested, I'll be getting along now.' I picked up my string bag, thanked the two old ladies, bidding them farewell. Without a word more to the astonished military, I walked on.

That night I had a dream. I dreamt I was sitting in a classroom in front of a stern, old dragon-lady teacher from primary school. She was ringing a dull-sounding, clanking hand-bell. Simultaneously, I would ring a high-pitched, sonorous hand-bell. She would stop, scowl and commence to scold a boy without a bell. I found this very amusing and laughed heartily.

My subjective mind or unconscious self was letting me know that the golden thread, the key feeling which accompanied me through the embarrassment, humiliation, indignation, fear and stifled anger, was a roguish delight in 'foiling the foiler of his prey'. On further reflection, I was forced to admit to myself that I had carried a marked, studied copy of the Pope's letter on the theme of struggle against hunger knowing that the soldiers would pounce on this like ravenous wolves. Such zeal for the scouring of a papal pronouncement is not to be found in many Catholic circles.

Besides all this, deep within me, I know that my bell peals at a higher pitch than theirs.

PASCHAL FIRE
26th March 1989

THE EASTER VIGIL IS the most solemn celebration in the Church's calendar. On that night Light wrestles against the powers of darkness and defeats them. Darkness is banished. The fire of Christ rises Víctorious from the embers of death. Life is made new; fresh Spirit is breathed into a fallen world.

This detailed, orderly ceremony is rich in symbolism and charged with deep meaning. So, I was intent on 'getting it right' and not to bungle up the liturgy, as is my wont. The Paschal Candle is symbolic of Christ who conveys strong warmth that enlightens the darkness of the world. A villager moulded it from brown beeswax. It looked sturdy and compact.

The fire blazed in the porch. I pierced the candle with the five wounds of Christ in the shape of a cross. 'Christ today and for ever, our beginning and our end. Alpha and Omega.' Solemnly, I dipped the candle into the flames. The wick wouldn't catch fire. I held it longer in the flames and feigned patience. The beeswax dripped, and the wick refused to take fire.

Old Niña Juanita broke the silence and solemnity of the night by saying 'It's nylon.' I ignored the wisdom of the Ancients and asked for a knife to hew out a longer wick, but the wick melted into the wax, no matter how deep I cut. The Paschal Candle looked impressive on the outside, but its wick of nylon was useless for holding live flame.

Perhaps we, the Church, resemble the Paschal Candle of nylon wick. Often, we prove useless when it comes to holding the strong fire of Jesus Christ and conveying his fiery Gospel to the world. We reject his destructive, divisive flame.

> 'I came to bring fire to the earth and how I wish it were burning now. Don't think I came to bring peace to the earth; I came not to bring peace but the sword.' (Luke 12:49; Matthew 10:34)

THE PEACE PROPOSAL
April 1989

> When Jesus was nearing Jerusalem he saw the city and
> shed tears for it, and he said, 'Would that today you
> too might understand the ways of peace. But they are
> things that you can't see at present. There will come
> days for you, in which your enemies will dig trenches
> around you; they'll attack you; they'll hem you in
> on every side. They'll trample you into the soil, you
> and your children, who live within your walls, and
> they won't leave in you one stone on top of another,
> because you have not recognised the appropriate time
> nor the arrival of God.' (Luke 19:41-44)

IT WAS SLIGHTLY IRKSOME. The radio, television and press
were interrupted ad nauseam by Arena's campaign advertising.
This political party can well afford to pour millions into election
propaganda. A lot of it was material attacking the governing
Christian Democrats (PDC). For instance, the television advert
where a light bulb swings in a dark room. A little girl wearing her
nightgown appears and says, 'Mummy, I'm hungry.' Her mother
hugs her and answers, 'Don't worry, dear, the PDC have lost the
elections.' 'Vote Arena' comes onto the screen.

A few days later another advert of a dark room and a light
bulb counters this. A different girl in her nightgown appears and
says, 'Mummy, I'm scared.' Her mother hugs her and answers,
'Don't worry, dear, Arena have lost the elections.' 'Vote PDC'
comes onto the screen.

Arena accuses PDC of being thieves who, in their term of
government, stole money earmarked for the relief of the poor.
The PDC meanwhile accuse Arena of being the Death Squad party
and of being responsible for the murder of the poor. Perhaps
both parties are correct in their assertions. I remember a wily old
campesino grinned when asked about the elections. 'You can't

replace a snake with a tiger,' he remarked, shaking his head.

In the course of this Salvadorean election campaign, President Reagan (whom some say showed a bland exterior, a sluggish mind and a hawkish heart during his presidency) handed over office to George Bush. Three days later the Guerrilla judged the time to be ripe and, on 23rd January, they proposed to the United States government, the political parties of El Salvador, the PDC and its Armed Forces, that the elections due to be held on the 19th of March be postponed until 15th September. The Joint High Command of the FMLN Guerrilla stated that if these elections were internationally supervised, clean, and free of military coercion, then they would put the bases of their political support behind Guillermo Ungo's Democratic Convergency Party and abide by the results. This would effectively end the nine years of war and bloodshed which has ravaged tiny El Salvador.

This offer was initially rejected without serious consideration by the PDC's cancer-ridden President Duarte and by those who put personal and political power and wealth before peace for the people. Realising the bad publicity which his initial rejection had created, Duarte hesitated and said it would be discussed further. His eventual proposal was to stage elections at the end of April, thus making propaganda for himself and his party as being seemingly flexible and working toward peace. This counter-proposal, however, wouldn't allow sufficient time for the FMLN and the Socialist Coalition to organise their bid for political power. The FMLN Guerrilla and Arena refused to accept Duarte's play for April elections and the elections took place on the date fore-planned.

On Sunday 19th March, amidst Guerrilla attacks on towns and villages and the boycott which forbade the movement of any traffic on the roads, incomplete elections took place. Many were unable to vote, given the circumstances, and many refused to vote, deeming these elections with their heavy military vigilance as being farcical.

In 1984, before Napoleón Duarte became President, he

promised to bring peace to the country. In his term of office, he and his party failed to produce any effective peace plan or hold realistic negotiations with the Guerrilla. The presidential candidate of the PDC was Fidel Chávez Mena, a lawyer for the Oligarchy, and a rather colourless character with a monotone voice.

After the elections, I had a dream which reflected my personal impression of the PDC during its years of Government. Chávez Mena, normally spruce with a spick and span suit, was lying propped up against a wall, drunken. His dress was shabby, his face unshaven. Then I saw a funeral scene where there were three small light-brown coffins joined as one, hewn from one block of wood. And, separately, there was the coffin of Chávez Mena. Swiftly the scene changed back to the inebriated Chávez Mena slumped on the floor. He slurred the words, 'I killed my children. That was the last act I committed before killing myself.'

History may well affirm that Napoleón Duarte and the PDC were guilty not only of grand-scale corruption, but also of genocide. And the three-in-one of the children's coffins symbolised the Three-in-One of the Christian Trinity. The history of the Church in years to come may well accuse the PDC of theocide – killing God in his Poor.

Arena won the March elections with a majority of popular support. It's calculated that, of those Salvadoreans eligible to vote, only one in six want Arena to govern. The one-sixth of the total voting population is that made up of the rich and powerful sector of Salvadorean society. The Party's official leader and President-elect is Alfredo Cristiani, a rich coffee merchant, but its founder and principal motivator is Major Roberto D'Aubuisson. D'Aubuisson is unacceptable as official leader by the U.S. government, because he is alleged to be the intellectual assassin of Archbishop Óscar Romero nine years ago, and the co-ordinator of the notorious death-squads which have murdered thousands of people. The people wait with fear and apprehension for Arena to take full control of government in

June. The Guerrilla are calling for a popular insurrection and are building towards that. Meanwhile, it looks certain that President Bush's administration will continue to send military aid to the Armed Forces and the Arena Government. A proposal of peace, a sign of hope, has been offered by the Guerrilla and discarded by politicians, and the people continue to suffer the consequences of this nine-year-old civil war.

THE DEATH OF A MENTALLY RETARDED CHILD
25th May 1989

'I will never forget you.' (Isaiah 49:156)

RAIN SWEPT DOWN FROM the darkened skies. The streets were muddy, the stones slippery, as we walked to bid farewell to Manuel de Jesús. He was thirteen years of age when he died, having spent the last three days of his life vomiting water. The cause of his death is unknown.

We entered the house where the people were gathered, ready to celebrate the customary all-night wake. The child's remains had been placed on the table and covered with a heap of flowers. Two candles burned beside him. One nostril of Manuel's nose was crudely blocked with cotton wool, and on his head they had put what seemed to me a rather comical, paper party hat, supposedly cut in the shape of a crown. I sat down beside Don Tavo, the child's father.

'I tell you, that child drew tears from me when he died at one o'clock this morning,' Don Tavo told me. 'He left behind a lot of fond memories.'

'You were always together, Don Tavo,' I said. 'You were even always at Mass together.'

'Yes,' he replied, 'we were always together . . . At night time, before he went to sleep, he used to giggle aloud when I made the sign of the cross over him. I would take his hand in mine and trace the cross from his forehead to his breast, then to his shoulders. Then he'd hug me and smother me with kisses. Manuel was mentally retarded, but he was full of affection. He was our only child . . . He liked to go to church. He liked the music. He used to walk to the sacristy and bring out a guitar and strum away at a chord. He knew how to keep beat with the music, clapping his hands, stamping his foot . . . Last week I took him with me to sow the fields. He got hold of my machete-sickle, dug a hole and put a few grains in it . . . You know, Manuel would never take supper until I came home from the fields, then we'd both sit down and eat together . . . He was our only child, and now he's gone. I'll miss him.'

SUNT LACRIMAE RERUM
19th June 1989

I caught up with the funeral procession weaving its weary way over the mountain paths to the cemetery. The mourners were surprised to see me, but I had anointed Niña Menches with the oils of the sick a few months previously and, for me, she typified the sorrow and hardship borne by the rural women of El Salvador; I wanted to pay my respects. Poor she lived, and poor she died. Menches had been dying of cancer for four years, and her long, painful journey to Calvary often made her feel dispirited. But she was free now, her voyaging over.

On the journey to the graveyard Don Francisco, her husband, explained, 'She began haemorrhaging after she gave birth to this child.' He carried on his shoulders a shy, barefooted, grubby child wearing a laughing Woody Woodpecker tee-shirt. 'After Paquito's birth four years ago, she was diagnosed as having cancer of the womb, and that's what caused her death. She was bedridden the last few days of her life.'

The brown-painted coffin fastened to poles was borne on the shoulders of two of the men. It was a heavy burden which chafed their collar bones, and they occasionally stopped to rest and change personnel. On one such stop, I noticed a scrawny, bony, black and white puppy sniff the side of the coffin, her tail limp between her hind legs, her lively eyes darting glances to each of us, puzzled and searching for the meaning of all this.

At the cemetery a few of the men swung shovel and hoe, digging deep into the earth. They delayed two hours more before their task was completed. I don't mind this, because powdered orange drink and cake were served at the graveside and I wolfed down my breakfast gratefully. I then took to jesting and made Estelina, Menche's ten-year-old daughter, laugh. Her friends joined in the buffoonery as I pulled funny faces and made them jump down from the white, cemented tomb where we stood on to the grass below. It was as good a way as any of passing the time.

'May the choirs of angels receive you and, in the company of Lazarus, poor in this life, may you have everlasting repose.'

We finished the graveside prayer and the soil was cast onto the coffin. I watched little Paquito's solemn face as he stared down at the spade digging and digging and digging into the orange clay. His mother had gone away. Soon he would be taken to San Salvador and reared by an aunt. His beltless trousers drooped, showing his bare, slightly swollen tummy. An ashen-faced Estelina held the wooden cross which would mark the place of burial for her mother's mortal remains. A stultified Don Francisco stood between his two youngest children carrying in his hand a lit candle. The dull, monotonous slicing of the spade against the earth broke the silence.

Later in the day, as I walked to the next village, the winter rains began to fall. Rivulets of water quickly formed along the path, streaming through the slippery orange mud. The rain beat tempo against the brim of my straw hat as I reflected on the day's events. Three Latin words of the Roman poet, Virgil, drummed through my mind 'Sunt lacrimae rerum'. 'These are the tears of things.' 'Sunt lacrimae rerum.'

LITTLE FRANCISCO
20th July 1989

'Greed thieves, wounds, and sucks blood. The greedy person has no heart in his breast. He sees not the anguish of tears. He feels no pity. His hands run with blood, blood of the poor, the widows, the orphans. His clothing is woven of robbery and plunder. His opulence is his condemnation.

'Where do their riches come from? From thieving and fraudulence. What is owed in justice cannot be stifled by alms or "charity". They do no more than give of what does not belong to them. They are only administrators of their goods. Their duty is to put their possessions at the service of the common good.'

THESE ARE WORDS PREACHED by St Antony of Padua more than seven hundred and fifty years ago. I was quoting this teaching of Antony in the Eucharist of the 29th of April. To illustrate the point of not cheap charity but total justice I drew a ten centavo coin from my pocket and cast it jingling across the temple floor. Three-year-old Francisco, who was sitting on the ground, crawled towards the coin and grasped it tightly in his tiny hand. This scene amused me, and I thought how it would have amused St Antony, that man of deep learning and great simplicity, who was the friend of the poor and the children. In fact, the peasant children sobbed and wept profusely when the thirty-six-year-old saint died.

On the 22nd of June I met Francisco outside the church, his jockey cap perched on his blond, curly head of hair. I greeted him and asked if he would gift me a curl. He looked at me with an intense seriousness and replied, 'Only if you give me money . . .'

I laughed, and visualised young Francisco developing into a prosperous businessman, conducting complicated transactions with economic skill and astuteness. He might even become a Celebrator of the Word like his father, respected by the community, a leader. But this was not to be. On the night of the 5th of July, three days after sustaining grievous burns by tipping over a boiling cauldron of milk, he died. His burns were major, and he couldn't be transported the long journey to hospital for fear that he should die on the way.

'I'm okay now,' he pleaded, weeping, to his older brother, not bearing the touch of ointment on his tender, reddened skin. His father had journeyed to La Palma seeking medical advice. The doctor could do no more than recommend hospitalisation, but the child breathed his last breath and passed on.

In heaven, the tonsured St Antony may well wish to buy a golden curl from Francisco's array of locks. But it will cost him dear.

BACK TO SQUARE ONE
1st August 1989

IN THE BOARD GAME of snakes and ladders the dice may fall badly for the thrower and force him or her to return to the beginning.

The coyote is a wild dog that roams the hills. It's also the word used to describe the illegal travel agent who pockets your $1,000 USA and promises to lead you north to the Promised Land of the United States of America. Many Salvadoreans go with the coyote. A lot seem to make it through the border and into safety, but many, like Víctor, are unlucky. They are caught, have their money unofficially confiscated by corrupt policemen, and are forced to return to El Salvador.

Víctor looked pale and drawn.

'They sent you back?' I said to him.

'Yes. I got caught in Mexico, in a border town,' he replied. 'It was the last stage of the journey. The Mexican coyote was due to take us the final stretch to Los Angeles. Two of us were given instructions to wait for our contact in a certain public park. It happened to be crawling with Customs Police, and there we were in the middle of them. We waited four hours and the coyote still didn't show up. The policemen got suspicious and arrested us at six-thirty in the evening.'

'Did they beat you up?' I wondered.

'No,' Víctor replied, 'But my friend had a Mexican identity letter. He had previously spent eight years working in Mexico. They wanted to know the source that produced the letter for him and came down hard. In the bus station he showed me the bruises on his ribs. They took most of our money from us.

'It had been difficult up till then. In one place forty of us were hidden in a small room. Someone fingered us to the authorities. We had to get dressed fast and clear out of there at midnight. A police car patrolled, searching for us. We had to spend two nights sleeping rough in the hills, because they were combing the area in pursuit. The girls wept a lot. We were all afraid, but it affected them more than us. We tried to console them.

'My family were waiting for me in Los Angeles and were pretty worried when I didn't turn up. They had employment arranged for us . . .

'It's not for the money that I want to go to the States. I've no material ambitions. It's just that if they pick you up here, in a bus queue, they force you to join the Army. And it doesn't take long before you get maimed or killed . . . One lad slit his wrist to avoid being taken by them. Others pretend they're mentally retarded.'

'The Army has a system of forced recruitment. We've had quite a few cases of that in past weeks,' I said. 'I hope your luck holds out better next time, Víctor, and that you reach LA.'

THE SONG OF THE POOR
8th August 1989

SOCIOLOGICALLY, IT IS INCORRECT to consider the Poor
of El Salvador as a homogeneous mass, because there are three
classes of Poor existing side by side in rural Chalatenango, to use
that area as an example.

The Bourgeois Poor
Economically, these may be among the poorest of the poor,
but their mentality is akin to that of the ruling classes. In the
community they domineer, often using a church position of
'mayordomo' (organiser of a village feast) as a subtle means of
maintaining social prestige. At the time of the feast they make
a customary collection, carrying a statue of the saint from door
to door. They keep no written account of these takings which
makes one suspect corruption.

Young girls are often 'hired' by them to mill corn, make
meals, wash clothes, sweep the house and look after the children.
In return for slavery the girls are given their meals and a hammock
to sleep in. They receive no wages. In this aspect the Bourgeois
Poor ape the rich who keep lowly paid household maids in their
mansions situated in the wealthy sectors of San Salvador.

Whether through conviction, fear or greed, individuals
of this sector often receive paid espionage assignments from
the military. Their task is to inform on Guerrilla positions and
to name Guerrilla sympathizers living in the communities. If
these people are arrested, investigated, and found guilty by the
Guerrilla, they are often executed by firing squads.

The Dormant Poor
This sector of the Poor avoids any political commitment in the
civil war and adopts an 'antiseptic' posture. 'Neither one band
nor the other,' they claim. For them, all violence is equally evil,
including the violence of self-defence against an unjust aggressor.

They interpret 'turn the other cheek' as passive non-violence, not as an instruction against vengeance. They often take refuge in a gnostic Christ-above-humanity spirituality. They lament their poverty but lack a spirit of struggle to improve their standard of living. 'We must conform ourselves to God's will,' they tell you as their malnourished sick child slips nearer death. Stoically they resign themselves to their child's death. It's not in them to walk, carrying their infant, to the nearest clinic and there demand medical assistance for her. They fear co-operatives and trade unions as being political commitment and are reluctant to denounce any violation of their rights as human beings.

The Poor with Spirit

These are a different breed from the other two categories. They are alive and spirited, a people aware of their chains. They are conscious of their material poverty, their subhuman misery, and seek to be free of it. Reluctantly they acknowledge the sad necessity, in certain situations, of using collective violence in an act of self-defence. That's how they interpret the existence of the Guerrilla and the state of civil war. They view politics as the positive means of promoting greater sharing and social justice for the workers. They denounce any violation of their rights as human beings. They suffer persecution, torture, and death from the military. These are the Poor who have a song to sing.

THE DEATH OF CHRIST
14th August 1989

NIÑA JULIA, A WRINKLED, wizened widow, looked at me expectantly as I made to walk past her house. I smiled, hesitated, greeted her and, changing direction, walked towards her.

The poor who have become old often exude tranquillity, a silent stillness in their eyes, a demeanour which expresses a journey through suffering. The Swiss psychoanalyst, Carl Jung, would possibly describe this maturity as the final stage of the individuation process, a rounding off of the personality. Be as it may, their deep calmness evangelises me more than a thousand theological tomes.

Niña Julia made me welcome and hastily put a sheet of newspaper on the wooden bench which had become ingrained with dirt over the years. She asked me to sit down.

In the course of our conversation I inquired about her husband. Her reply took me aback. 'They killed him eight years ago. We had moved out of the village and were living in San Salvador. People started making false accusations against my husband, and he was put on a wanted list. There was a time in this village when people spoke evil with their tongue. My husband was informed of their accusations and decided to travel to San Francisco and clear his name with the Civil Defence. It was evening, and darkness was falling when the lorry arrived. He didn't even have time to descend when they approached and arrested him. They took him captive to the outskirts of the village and tied him with a rope to a tree. Then they poured paraffin over his body and set him alight. He screamed in agony and they shot him twice through the head. They kicked his body down a ditch and left him there. Andrés, a friend, found the body next day.'

She then told me how she had returned to San Francisco Morazán after the murder of her husband, because she had been born in this place and here was where she had her home. 'Those who took part in the killing still live here,' she said, pointing to the house opposite. And she named four ex-members of the Civil Defence. Her tone of voice bore sadness, but not resentment.

'It must be very painful for you, meeting your husband's killers in the street,' I remarked.

'I talk to them,' she answered. 'With God there is forgiveness.'

She said this not sanctimoniously, but with a matter-of-fact simplicity while averting her gaze from mine.

'Your husband died the same death as Christ, an innocent victim tied to a tree. And the same as Archbishop Romero ....' I felt myself to be in the presence of sanctity and, like Peter the Apostle, I mouthed words too shallow to describe the reality being experienced. 'Yes,' she nodded, 'my husband died the same death as Christ and Archbishop Romero.'

SONYA
23rd September 1989

'HOW WAS THE SLOPE, then?' she asked with a broad smile. I looked at her, this small girl guerrilla, chubby without being fat, brown hair and brown, sparkling eyes which met mine. Rather fetching, I thought. 'The slope was pretty serious business,' I panted, my head nodding exaggeratedly. Her smile burst into a good-natured chuckle. The first hill had been climbed and sweat trickled down my face and soaked my tee-shirt.

Our conversation turned to the latest political happenings in the country, namely the dialogue and negotiation which had begun between the Government and the Guerrilla. We spoke of the unilateral cease-fire declared by the Guerrilla and the People's Independence Day March for Peace to take place in the capital.

The clopping of a mule's hooves descending from among the pine trees and heading in our direction made me feel a little uncomfortable. It is not advisable for the priest to be seen by civilian population fraternising with the Guerrilla, even if these three guerrillas had been the ones who had suddenly appeared from the trees and stopped us in our tracks and initiated conversation. An elderly man rode the beast, leading by the reins another mule saddled but riderless. At the rear of this single-file procession was a woman labouring under a heavy white sack of corn which was balanced on her head.

'Hey,' Sonya shouted to the woman, 'why don't you put that sack on the saddle?' The rider made himself deaf to this suggestion and sauntered on. 'Do you hear what I'm saying?' repeated the armed maiden. 'Let her put that sack on the mule's back.' But the rider paid her no heed and continued his journeying. We watched them proceed into the distance.

'That bundle can damage the woman's neck muscles,' I remarked. 'Such is the fate of the Salvadorean woman.' She agreed with me.

Sonya spoke with revolutionary pride about the recent spate of activities conducted by the urban Guerrilla in San Salvador. I paused, looked at her with a smile and said, 'You're a hard wee soul.' She found this comment funny and chuckled with great glee, trying to deny her combative toughness.

'Well, I don't want to hold you back any longer,' she said. I fished a bag of bread out of my net bag and offered it to them. 'No, you eat it,' she said, refusing my offer. 'I've got two bags of bread with me,' I coaxed. 'Okay, then,' she said, accepting the bread. Our unorthodox Communion Service completed, we bade farewell with warm friendliness and took to the trail once more.

'Do take care,' I reminded them.

Four days after this encounter with Sonya, she was shot dead by soldiers' bullets while convening a political meeting with the people of Los Sitios, Dulce Nombre de María. Later, on discovering that they had killed a rebel authority figure, the troops disinterred her mortal remains from the grave the people had given her and snapped their macabre propaganda photographs.

Today the rain falls tearfully to the earth. A purple flower lies trampled in the mud, its soft petals severed and broken. But another will surely bloom and take its place in the ebb and flow of life. And, one day, the people will be free.

QUEEN OF THE ROAD
9th October 1989, Tegucigalpa, Honduras

THE TARMAC ROAD RUNNING parallel to the airport seemed to sizzle in the mid-day sun. Dust clogged breathing space and we felt relieved to enter the gaudy, antiseptic, orange plastic, American-styled Big Burger restaurant at the side of the road. The fan blew clear air, refreshing our weary bones before our flight departed in three hours.

Slowly and thankfully we sipped our ice-cold Cola drinks and gazed out into the haze. Then plodding towards us came three scruffy children. Fresh and streetwise, they grinned at us. 'Hey, gives a drink of your Coke, eh,' quipped the youngest boy.

'No,' intervened the eldest sister sagely, 'Don't listen to him; he's always trying to screw people.'

Her smile captivated and I invited the two sisters and their youngest brother to partake of a cold Coke with us. Their grins broadened and a gleam appeared in their eyes as they passed noisily to a table in the plastic palace protected by uniformed, commercial sentinel. The odour of their sweat wafted through the premises. Alerted, a frowning personnel manager approached, intending to eject this jetsam of society to the outer part of the ring, back to where they belong. But we spoke on behalf of our invited guests, stating that they were awaiting their order of Cola. The manager backtracked submissively while the children's faces beamed delight. The oldest girl, the Queen of the Road, looked as if she had been gifted a million dollars whereas, in reality, she was only sitting for a while on a forbidden orange plastic seat of the Gringo inner sanctum, waiting on an ice-cold Cola.

In the eyes of God – if God has eyes – these rough-talking, uncouth children would be the most important people present in the world of the Big Burger. More prestigious than you, more prestigious than me. They own the Kingdom of God, although they could never hope to own the world of the Big Burger.

THE WOUND OF LOSS
14th December 1989

'¿Adónde te escondiste, Amado
Y me dejaste con gemido?
Como el ciervo huiste,
habiéndome herido.
¡Salí tras tí clamando,
Y eras ido!'
St John of the Cross

OFTEN I'VE SAT EATING tortilla and frijol beans in the house of Niña Juana and Don Lucio. Before the meal is set on the table they perform the ritual of scaring the household pig from the porch into the courtyard. 'Cuche!' is the word of exorcism uttered at the fat swine as he scampers to avoid flying footwear. Unfortunately, the flea-bitten dog, the flat-footed duck and the ginger cat are never evicted, and they remain to keep me company as I try self-consciously to ignore their begging animal eyes.

'I had a son who died seven years ago. Would you pray for him in today's Mass?' asked Niña Juana.

'Sure,' I replied, 'What's his name?'

'Lucio Cruz Varela, the same name as his father. I have a photograph.'

She went to the back room and brought out a framed photograph of her deceased son. It was an enlargement of his miniature identity document photo. I sat looking at him. He had closely cropped hair and square-set jaws and his shoulders seemed brawny.

'Was he a soldier?'

'Yes,' answered the dead soldier's mother. 'He was twenty-seven years of age and recently married when he was shot dead in an ambush near Arcatao.'

The photograph was a representation of her son. It brought back to her memories of the baby she had suckled at her breast and watched grow through the years. Because of war, he was now lost for ever.

Today, the fourteenth of December, is the feast of St John of the Cross, our village patron. This tiny Carmelite friar, who lived over four hundred years ago in Spain, wrote deeply moving poetry from his prison cell. In the darkness of the dungeon John of the Cross was made to endure cruel whiplashing inflicted by a group of Carmelite colleagues who resented his attempts at religious reform. His poetry was born out of a heartrending quest for his beloved God in the midst of human suffering and despair. A recurring theme in the mystical John of the Cross's writing is the wound of loss borne as a result of separation from the Beloved. This search for his dearly loved departed One was a harrowing experience for the friar. And the mother's heartbreak on losing her child is a similarly harrowing experience.

> 'Where are you hidden, my loved One?
> You've left me groaning.
> You fled like a deer
> causing me woundedness.
> I went after you crying,
> but you were gone.'

Sitting looking at the photograph of a now deceased soldier, I felt a kind of compassion for the dead man and his family. Something stirred in my soul despite an admitted personal aversion to the Salvadorean Army. War always brings sorrow to the poor, and the loss of their loved ones will always cut them to the quick.

WHAT THE DICKENS
4th November 1989

IT IS NO LITTLE accomplishment finding a secondhand bookshop in Central America that stores a few English language classics. But, in Guatemala last Eastertide, I discovered such a place.

I felt pleased at being able to buy a copy of Charles Dickens' *Dombey and Son*, and happily I sauntered out of the shop with the book clasped under my right armpit. As a youth, I had read most of Dickens' classics, but I had never got round to reading *Dombey and Son*. This copy was in paperback and the yellowish pages were only just beginning to wilt at the edges. It was to be a treat to relish, feeding my mind with Dickens while ambling around the verdant, high-altitude communities of the parish.

Dombey and Son got pride of place on the shelf of our log cabin in Yerba Buena. It was being conserved as a delicacy to whet my spiritual appetite, and I intended delving into its pages at the earliest opportunity after completing Melville's *Mardi* and Tolstoy's *War and Peace*. But it was not to be.

This morning I raised the plastic dust cover off the bookshelf and pulled out *Dombey and Son* – just to feel its texture between my fingers and browse over its pages with my eyes.

The earlier section had been gnawed to shreds and on touch it disintegrated further. Hundreds of printed letters of this famous classic were piled into a soft, cushioned mound inside the fly cover.

Stricken, uttering disbelief, I walked out of the hut, cradling the dead pieces in the palms of my hands. The Niña Laura, unaware of the sheer magnitude of the catastrophe, stopped brushing and glibly remarked, 'Look what a mouse has done to the Bible.'

I grimaced and thought, 'My dear, this is more serious.' We have several copies of Holy Writ, but there was only one extant English version of Dickens' *Dombey and Son* in the whole of Chalatenango. What's more, I deem it wholly unnatural that a mouse should have a taste for Dickens.

BANTER
30th December 1989

I MEANDERED DOWN THE grass verge to the house where I was to be given supper. In the house was old Don Expectación, seated on the bench, holding court before the others. I arrived in the middle of his patter.

'Padre, what do you think? Can I get married?' His impish grin revealed the gap between decayed teeth.

'Don Expectación, you already are married — to Niña Florinda.' I smiled.

He guffawed with uncontrolled merriment. 'But I want to know if I can get married again?'

'Well,' I mused, 'You can, but it wouldn't be right.'

He found this answer very funny and burst out laughing once more.

Expectación is one of the poorest people in the village. He and his family had been displaced from their place of origin because of the war. His peasant clothing was typically shabby, but his old straw hat was perched on a happy head. The old man held, blade down, his machete, the rural instrument of toil, pointing it to the earthen floor.

I quipped, 'If I were you, Don Expectación, I'd watch out. These young girls are only after your money.'

More humour and laughter ensued. The grey shadow of evening was slowly, almost imperceptibly, covering the village, and being as in the morning there had been bombing and gunfire owing to the army presence in the surrounding hills, the old man thought it wise to excuse himself and head off for home.

'I'll be looking out for you at Mass tomorrow, Don Expectación,' I remarked, feeling a little like an old Irish parish priest. 'And bring along your wife, not the girlfriend.'

Still laughing amiably, the old man ambled home to the warmth of the kitchen fire, where awaited him his faithful spouse.

1990

GIVE SORROW WORDS
January 1990

'And I – if I lose you, it would be better for me to go down into my grave. There will be no more comfort for me if you are taken, but only sorrow . . . Pity me and stay behind the walls; do not make your boy an orphan and your wife a widow.' (Homer, *The Iliad*, Bk VI)

Grieve. Cry. Sigh.
Let fall the tears
Let flow those rivulets of melancholy.
The eyes are the index of the mind
And your gentle mind has been broken by death.
So don't stifle grief and pain.
Scream. Shout.
Gush out the rage and tempest.
Your loved one has been slain.
Never more will you hear his footfall
Return from labour in the maize field,
Or run your tender fingers through his tousled hair.
Never more will the warm hearth pulsate
with the security of his laughter.
In future years
he will not be there
to sooth your stress
and calm your fears.
He is gone for ever,
bled to death
on a battlefield.
Left lonely,
widowed with crying children
that clutch and cling

to your threadbare dress.
He, strong companion, father of your offspring
has departed, and is no more.
How on earth will you buy food
since you have no money?
Woman plunged in poverty and loss,
despair and dark deep struggle
will be your lot
in the years to come.

He is gone for ever,
bled to death
on a battlefield.

THE SONS OF CAIN
January 1990

I WAS HURRYING TO reach Chacones before nightfall. It is not wise to be walking the mountain paths of Chalatenango after nightfall. The Psalmist does warn against the 'Terror that prowls in the darkness' and counsels caution not to 'strike your foot against a stone' (Psalm 91).

What I saw ahead on the Los Naranjos path was disturbing. Two young men were squaring up to one another like prize-fighting cocks. Each threatened to strike the first blow. Both were reeling drunk. Toño grasped in his right fist a 'corvo' which is a straight, sharp yard-long, stainless steel blade. A corvo is an instrument for work in the fields, but when a group of men patrol the village, inebriated with firewater on a Sunday evening, the corvo becomes a lethal weapon. Toño's opponent in the pink tee-shirt carried a half brick in his hand and, on a grass verge above them, stood the judges of the contest – about a half dozen men, all drunk, and all wielding corvos. Daniel Ardón, whom I had helped escape execution by the Guerrilla in November 1987, was prominent among them.

I arrived on the scene, 'What are you doing?' I asked.

'We're making sure they don't hurt one another,' lied Ardón.

'Don't be fighting,' I told them. 'Why don't you go off home for some supper and some sleep?'

'Don Tomás, are you trying to fuck me up? If you are, come on then!' shouted Toño challengingly.

'Hey, don't you menace me,' I answered. 'We're friends. I'm not trying to fuck you up. Nobody is trying to fuck you up. Shake hands.'

I did not want to rile a drunk man with a lethal weapon and I wanted him to remove his corvo from his right hand, even for a few brief moments. Then I coaxed Toño's opponent to drop his half brick and shake Toño's hand. Then I asked the opponent to go home. He just stood there, sozzled.

'Don Tomás are you trying to fuck me up?' repeated Toño, brandishing his corvo.

'No, we're friends, remember,' I said. 'Why not go home to your wife?'

Once more, I asked the opponent with the pink tee-shirt to go home, but he just stood there, sozzled.

'Don Tomás, may the Lord give you many women to love,' slurred Toño. I reflected silently that my friend Toño had imparted a very nice blessing for me.

Seeing that the opponent was unwilling to take his opportunity and move from the scene I decided to leave them. If need arose I am prepared to die for the people, but I am not prepared to sacrifice my life for the whim of belligerent drunkards. I left them hoping that my act of presence may have proved a sobering influence. In fact, I later learned that nobody was wounded in this exchange.

Braggart drunkards wielding weapons are not an infrequent sight in Salvadorean village life. A while ago I met a man, who had once confessed murder, wielding his machete in a drunken state. This man had wept bitter tears under the tamarind tree as he recalled the murder in cold blood ten years previously. Then, months later, the penitent appeared drunk, grasping his machete and shouting abusive language. He did not aim his aggression directly at me, but I felt bad vibrations coming in my direction, especially when he hacked at a fence-post five yards away. Possibly the sensation I experienced was similar to that of the fainting Freud whose intuition perceived Jung to possess an evil-eye death-wish against him, hidden in Jung's subconscious 'id'. Quietly, I excused myself and walked away, hearing the drunk's accusatory remarks that I was walking out on their company.

Remorse is a worm that eats away the soul. Those who have slain the poor and the defenceless must bear an intolerable burden till the day they die and, who knows, perhaps further. Only God can forgive them.

'With the Lord there is mercy and fullness of redemption.
And he will redeem Israel from all its iniquity.' (Psalm 130)

DOGGY GO HOME
31st January 1990

I LOOKED BEHIND ME on the dirt-track leading from San Francisco Morazán to Tremedal. A dog was dogging my footsteps. I stopped dead in my tracks and looked at him. The dog also stopped and, cocking his head inquiringly at me, wagged his tail back and forth.

'Go home,' I ordered, pointing a finger in mandatory fashion towards San Francisco Morazán.

'Go home,' I repeated in Spanish and again in English, for good measure. But I may as well have told the dog in my best juridical dog Latin, 'Cane, ite ad domum'. He merely ignored my every protestation and continued to follow me, his tail wagging.

I felt a little frustrated but rejected the notion of making my point with stones.

On arriving in Tremedal I entered the first house and the dog trotted faithfully behind me. I apologised to the people and explained that the shaggy beast had dogged my steps from San Francisco Morazán and that I had been unsuccessful in turning him back.

'Oh, that's alright, Padre,' the woman answered. 'It's our dog.'

A CANDLE FOR CHICO
18th February 1990

WHEN THEY TOLD ME that Chico (whose war name was 'Cheque') had been killed in a shoot-out with the Army, Old Sister Sadness came to settle once more in the inner recesses of my soul. It was sad news indeed.

He of the far-off gaze and the sardonic smile, father and husband with six young children, president of the village co-operative until he was arrested several times by the military and tortured on each occasion. Chico, the smouldering volcano, who took to the hills in defence of his people, is dead.

I remember last year when the village water pipe burst, high on the hills, he headed the repair team. At mealtime he shared his tin of sardines and tortillas with me, and on the return journey a plane hovered above us and Chico aimed the big red spanner at it, claiming he was wielding the latest Russian model, an AK47 rifle. On the last morning of January, he and two companions were surprised by an Army manoeuvre on their flank. A sharpshooter picked off his two companions, shooting a bullet through the neck of one and the head of the other. Chico was the only survivor and he radioed for instructions. 'I've got two dead with me,' he shouted over the walkie-talkie. Alicia, the girl commander, was incredulous and asked him to repeat what he was saying. He repeated it and she told him to retreat from the firing line. '¡Cachimbón!' he said. A phrase which could be translated as 'Bloody marvellous'. There were a few seconds of silence, then Alicia heard a loud spray of gunfire. Chico was dead.

He had spirit. He it was, as president of the Community's co-operative movement, who decided to expropriate the dormant lands of a wealthy villager. He it was who, in public, told greedy Don Emilio that he had enough property without snatching for his own use that of those who had fled the area.

Chico then invited the poor dispossessed to till and reap the harvest of those disused lands rent-free.

A few days before his death he expressed hurt that Daniel, who had been his friend, had stolen money earmarked for the 'war widows' and had fled into neighbouring Honduras. He lamented, 'The money can be replaced, but the friendship can't.'

I'll miss the blether, the dry crackling humour, the example of someone who put the struggle of his people before home comforts and personal safety.

Last night I sat alone in the darkness and lit a candle for Chico. I listened to Beethoven's *Missa Solemnis*. The words 'Crucifixus etiam pro nobis' haunted me. 'He was crucified for our sake.' I felt redeemed by the poor with spirit. They are the ones who are crucified for our sake. They are the Body of Christ we receive in the Eucharist. They shed their life blood in the hope of transforming society into something new, a place where justice and love can prevail over greed and hate. Chico and thousands of fellow Salvadoreans have been crucified for our sake. 'Crucifixus etiam pro nobis.'

The sombre melody of Beethoven's *Missa Solemnis* flooded the candlelit air. Slowly, I sipped my whisky and silently thanked God for Chico and those whose blood redeems us.

AN EMMAUS WALK
24th February 1990

IT WAS EARLY MORNING and I walked glumly towards San Francisco Morazán from San Rafael, a distance of four kilometres, taking over an hour to complete. On the road ahead old Don Félix hobbled at a tortoise's pace. I drew nearer, but he did not see me, his eyesight, like himself, was very poor. Félix walked with his old straw hat doffed to his chest, making the sign of the cross several times, whispering *sotto voce*. Maybe he was afraid. Fear impregnates the fibre of life in El Salvador. The vulnerable and defenceless often fall prey to military brutality with the soldiers accusing them of subversive activity.

Meeting old Félix deep in prayer on a lonely road was a moving experience. Maybe it could be described as being an experience akin to that undergone by the two disciples whom the death-defeating Christ accompanied along the Emmaus road. Meeting the vulnerable and weak Félix was for me a religious experience. I felt enlightened and moved by it. A bit like the frog that had been transformed into a prince.

We came face to face and he peered at me. I greeted him, he recognised my voice, and his face lit up into a smile.

'You're saying your prayers, Don Félix?' He nodded assent.

'You're an example to us all. I won't disturb you further.' I moved on.

The next morning, after the Sunday Eucharist, Félix approached and handed me a ten centavo coin. 'That's for the Blessed Sacrament,' he said with a smile. Obviously, he had made a promise to the Christ of the Eucharist to keep him safe on his journey and this was the fulfilment of his promise.

This ten centavos coin (equivalent to one penny sterling) has taken on a value beyond money. It is no longer ordinary currency. This particular coin has become a sacrament of the poor, a sign of simplicity, generosity and sacrifice. I intend to carry it with me as a sign of Christ, the Bread of Life.

TO THE
THORN-CROWNED
CHRIST

26th February 1990

Grip Caesar's mad bull by its horns.
Grasp the blood-red rose by its thorns.
Risk life.
Risk limb.
Feel fear and flinch, yes,
but stay steadfast come what may.
Wish resurrection
for the impoverished, death-smeared masses
and hope and hope and hope
till morning breaks the night
and justice be done.

THE TENTH ANNIVERSARY
24th March 1990

OVER THE PAST FEW DAYS the parish's main village has been heavily militarised by Government troops. Day and night, pockets of soldiers laze in doorways and pepper with their presence the forecourt and steps of the church. Earlier they had dealt out food parcels to the people in an effort to win popular support.

Being as the people of San Fernando Morazán in general tend to separate faith and social justice, I thought it would be appropriate to mark the tenth anniversary of Archbishop Romero's assassination with a morning celebration of the Eucharist. Christ's body broken on a cross, and his lifeblood poured out, a being sacrificed for the practice of truth, seemed a fitting expression of the life and death of Óscar Arnulfo Romero. This day should not pass unrecognised. The three northern repopulations of El Higueral, Teosinte and Tremedal had been invited to participate with us.

Imaginary butterflies tickled inside my tummy, because I knew that on this day there would be military surveillance on my preaching. Many in the military regard Archbishop Romero as having been a commander of the Guerrilla who deserved summary execution. No words can dissuade them from this rigid way of thinking. I suppose, there are none so blind as those who will not see.

I rang the three customary peals calling the people to worship, but only about fifteen people of San Francisco Morazán came, and these were mostly young girls and old women. I felt disappointed that so few parishioners wished to remember the words and sacrifice of Archbishop Romero, their pastor, their prophet, their martyr, who lives on in the hearts of the poor with spirit. Then from the sacristy I heard a stampede of feet and, peeping out, saw seventy-five people from the repopulations filing into the empty benches. There they were, a thrilling sight;

men, women and children, perspiring, carrying infants, the poor with spirit, some of them having walked nearly three hours to be present and they would repeat the journey to return. Ignoring the military's psychological pressure against commemorating Romero's memory they took their places at the table of the Lord.

In the sermon I took to developing a recent theme, the sign of Jonah, and applied its meaning to Monseñor Romero, without daring to mention the Jesuits recently murdered by the military. Needless to say, three officers stood at the back of the church, arms folded, listening. And at the point where I mentioned the sign of Jonah falling on Monseñor Romero, my first mention of his name in the homily, the senior officer turned on his heels and walked out, followed by the others. I continued, nervous but determined, emphasising that the centre of the Gospel message and the centre of Romero's preaching is the dignity of human life.

'Life is always sacred. The commandment of the Lord – "Thou shalt not kill" – makes the totality of life sacred, and blood spilt – even if it should be the blood of a sinner – always cries out to God. And those who kill are always guilty of homicide.

'As far as the church is concerned, there is nothing as important as human life, the human person. In particular, the persons of the poor and oppressed, which – besides being human – are also divine. That's why Jesus said that everything done to them He takes as done to Him. And that blood (blood, death) is beyond all politics. It touches the very heart of God.'

Preaching in El Salvador does require prudence, but the message of God's kingdom cannot honestly be accommodated to unjust structures. The military, like us all, have to serve and follow the Gospel. The Gospel should not be forced to serve and follow the military.

The sign of Jonah brought Jesus, Monseñor Romero and the Jesuit martyrs violent death. Nobody seeks that; it happens as a consequence of what one says and does. Martyrdom is not sought, it is encountered.

THE WINDS OF CONFLICT
4th April 1990

I SAT ON THE inside lane of the bus seats, next to old Don Sabino. Looking through the windowpane my eyes glimpsed young Lieutenant Hernández sitting on the steps of the circular cement bandstand in Dulce Nombre's main square. He was chatting amicably with the pretty schoolgirls who did not appear to be that much younger than him. They giggled, and he preened and combed back his black hair with an orange comb. A voice in my mind muttered an expletive and I screened my bearded face from view.

Don Sabino chatted about recent departures from this life. He sighed, 'All the old people are dying off. I'm bored with life; I just bide waiting my time to come to a close.'

'Come now, Don Sabino,' I reasoned, 'not all old people are dying off. You're not.'

He chuckled, 'I am, you know.'

In the background Lieutenant Hernández moved off with his chubby bodyguard shadowing him. A fleeting glance to the side and he took me in, and his features instinctively distorted. His head lowered like a wild bull and I could read the words formed on his lips doubting the legitimacy of my parents' marriage and my birth.

At the moment when the bus was pulling away he crossed the perimeter of the house's corridor and stood staring at me. I forced a smile and gave him a nod of acknowledgement. He gave me half a dozen condescending schoolmasterish nods in return, also forcing a smile. Then, he raised his left hand in a farewell (or good riddance) salutation and walked back to his comrades. I noted that his right forearm was lightly bandaged; perhaps this was a slight wound sustained during the rattle of bullets which had rung throughout the village on the previous night.

In the course of the past few weeks I've been involved in a

few confrontations with soldiers who have detained and menaced people from the repopulations of Tremedal and Teosinte as they passed through San Francisco Morazán. On one such occasion, Lieutenant Hernández aired suspicions regarding our pastorate, casting veiled aspersions that we are in allegiance with the Guerrilla. He also claimed that Fr Rutilio Grande, the Jesuit friend of Archbishop Romero, who was murdered thirteen years ago, had been an armed subversive. I refuted these allegations and when Hernández stated that an old woman of Teosinte had once refused him water and had threatened him with a cosh, I felt that this was bordering on the absurd. I dryly remarked, 'Lieutenant, Teosinte has a series of public taps with a continuous flow of fresh water, so why should you have to ask a villager for water instead of helping yourself?'

A few days later my colleague, Henry, had a few warning bullets shot across his path from hidden army snipers in nearby hills as he attempted the journey to Tremedal for the celebration of the Eucharist. He turned back but succeeded in arriving without mishap the following day.

Conflict in itself should never be sought, but in many instances of life it becomes inevitable. It would be nice not to have any enemies, but enemies crop up like tares in a wheatfield. It's a sobering thought, but if Jesus had managed to avoid conflict and not make enemies he would not have been killed on a cross.

GOLGOTHA
9th April 1990

IN THE MOONLIGHT THE songbirds perch among the branches, shielded by shivering foliage, and refuse to sing their song. Instead silence and deep sadness palls the air. A sense of foreboding falls on the world. It is as if humankind has tortured and killed the Godhead.

He was a factory worker, poor, stripped of dignity and material possessions. Just another nameless statistic in El Salvador, a nobody whose daily disappearance goes practically unannounced, and unnoticed, in the wilderness of death. You see, this trade union leader's thoughts and voice annoyed the powerful, so they beat his tiny brain to pulp and slit his throat, dumping his blood-drenched corpse in the waste heap. He thinks and talks no more. Take away the worker's mind, silence his voice and the ever swelling lake of private enterprise remains unrippled. We can all live in peace now, undisturbed by communists and traitors of the Fatherland. This worker demanded a greater proportion of labour's production, subverting society's order. Now he knows his place in life. His place is Golgotha.

TITO EL 'BOLO'
27th April 1990

IT SEEMS THAT ONLY when he scours the outskirts of the village searching for sticks is Tito not in a drunken stupor. Collecting and selling firewood is his way of earning coins to buy more firewater.

On one occasion, he managed to beg a few coins from Teosinte repopulators who were awaiting me in the presbytery corridor. I saw Tito take the coins and, knowing it was for alcohol, I approached and had to prise open his clenched fist in order to make him release and return the coins to the villagers. I explained that it was for the local hooch that he wanted their money and that he was going to kill himself of alcoholic poisoning as at least five other parishioners had done over the last four years. Instead of money, I gave him food and he scampered off like a lean cur biting a bone. Probably he bartered the food in exchange for *guaro* money, but it was important to have made a symbolic gesture against his suicidal habit. Maybe the sum of my life will be a series of futile gestures.

At other times the inebriated Tito saw me shopping for eggs and bread and aggressively demanded a share. I refused, knowing that this flyweight alcoholic wanted to convert bread or egg into alcohol for personal consumption.

During the week, I was sitting on the church steps waiting to ring the last peal before celebrating the evening Eucharist. Two soldiers passed by, pulling Tito, their prisoner. His thumbs were tied together behind his back. Another soldier followed behind, lending security at the rear.

Sighing, I stood up and walked towards them. 'Excuse me; you've made a mistake. We know this man. He's Tito, the local *bolo* [*id est*, drunk].' I wrongly thought they were accusing him of being a subversive.

On rounding the corner, one of the soldiers snappily demanded my identity documents stating, 'Nobody ... Nobody, be he father, mother, or whoever, has the right to impede the Armed Forces when they are making an arrest.'

I smiled at him, 'But I'm a Pastor and I've got a responsibility for the wellbeing of my sheep, even the black sheep. I know he's a drunk who spends his free time collecting firewood to exchange for drink ...'

'That's right,' intervened Tito, 'collect firewood to buy food.'

'To buy drink,' I corrected.

'Well, food too,' he muttered.

Under armed escort, we progressed to a place amongst a cluster of trees where the Lieutenant was seated, studying papers spread out upon the soil. He stood up when he saw me and courteously shook hands. In the course of the conversation Lieutenant Mancía ordered Tito's thumbs to be untied when I brought this to his attention. Apparently, Tito's father had denounced his son to the military, following a family quarrel. He had injured his father's hand and, consequently, the Lieutenant wanted to give Tito a warning. The prisoner was to be released after half an hour's good counsel.

Knowing the reason for the arrest, I agreed with the officer. 'A warning won't do him any harm, so long as he's not beaten up.'

He assured me there would be no physical violence done to Tito. We shook hands again and I took my leave.

After Mass, I glimpsed Tito the Bolo walking free down the main street, none the worse for his experience.

THE VALLEY OF THE FALLEN
24th May 1990

ON THE OUTSKIRTS OF Madrid there is a huge, underground mausoleum carved into a hillside. It was built to commemorate the slain of the Spanish civil war. Towering above this place is a huge stone cross. This is Spain's Valley of the Fallen. Gazing at the plain wooden cross on the hill overlooking Valle de Jesús, I'm reminded of the Valley of the Fallen because, in recent months, this village has been ravaged by El Salvador's civil war, and its people have experienced the irretrievable loss of loved ones.

Darkness enveloped us as we huddled into the church to celebrate the liturgy of sacrifice, the commemoration of a Palestinian carpenter who was flogged and nailed to die on wooden planks by the authorities of his day. The absence of sixteen members of the community killed in battle was felt deeply and this sentiment of sadness was emphasised by the fact that there was no musical accompaniment to the singing, because six of these men had been the players of the string instruments. Chico, Sergio, Juan Ángel, Margarito, Reyes and Esteban were all dead. The guitars, double bass and lyre lay dormant in the sacristy. To think that it was only sixteen months ago that I had officiated at Esteban's wedding. That was a happy occasion. Now, everything had changed; Carmen joins the long list of war widows with an uncertain future. Many village children are fatherless; their family provider gone for ever.

The absence of these young men was experienced deeply in the breaking of bread but, paradoxically, their presence was also accompanying us. The music of their love and example, their daring and sacrifice in the struggle for a just society, a better world for the poor, lives on. May their deaths not be in vain; may the seeds sown by their blood come to fruition. May there be peace based on social justice ('Pax opus iustitiae'), a peace which brings human dignity to society's scorned, a peace founded on the truth of the Gospel, a peace that lasts.

TITO'S THANK YOU
June 1990

IT WAS PENTECOST SUNDAY, a day of blasting wind, raging fire and sudden, total transformation – according to liturgical celebration but, as I sat on the steps of the church awaiting the arrival of the people, it felt like another humdrum Sunday. Then, out of the blue, struck a thunderbolt. Tito, a village drunk who had been arrested by the military and on whose behalf I had spoken, approached.

On the first Pentecost Sunday they accused the disciples of being sodden by alcoholic beverage. The truth of that is debatable but, beyond any shadow of doubt, Tito was a little intoxicated that Pentecost morning.

Melodramatically, he joined his hands, knelt in front of me, and made a solemn profession.

'Heavenly Father,' he slurred, giving me promotion to the sphere of the divine. 'You're my heavenly father. If you hadn't come and spoken a word for me the other day, then the fucking soldiers would have killed me.'

LAS CHICAS
8th June 1990

THE 'CHICAS' (OR THE 'Little Community' as they are also called) deny definition. Perhaps they could be described as a non-canonical religious group of young women who have taken vows of poverty, chastity and obedience to the people they serve, but not to any bishop or religious superior. They visit and catechise the poorer parishes of San Salvador, striving to further the kingdom of God on earth by their life option in favour of the poor.

These ten young women are full of fun and vitality. They laugh readily, brimming over with humour and good spirits. But what happened on Sunday 3rd June cast a dark shadow in their lives. In the early hours of that morning while they were all spending the night in their respective parishes, a military death squad used master keys to open their high iron gate and front door and enter. They ransacked the house, scattering personal belongings, archives and files. Nothing was apparently taken, but two blood-red crosses were painted on different walls in the inner part of the house. This was done as a symbol of warning and impending death. Also, a typewritten note was placed on the kitchen table.

Archbishop Rivera y Damas denounced this flagrant violation of religious liberty in his Sunday homily. Despite the start of fresh dialogue and negotiation for peace between the Guerrilla and the Government, the underlying atmosphere of threat and death squad activity prevails. Having seen the blood-red crosses marking the walls, and the signs of intrusion left behind in the home of these defenceless women religious who have been friends for a number of years, I felt my spine chill. The Beast that prowls in the dark threatens still.

Quantitatively, the murders and violations of basic human rights by the security forces (who sow insecurity) has decreased since the widespread genocide of the early eighties. Nonetheless, there can be no room for complacency, qualitatively the same hallmark murders and selective menacing activity persists. It was Hérbert Anaya, the non-governmental human rights leader, who first drew my attention to this quantitative/qualitative distinction in October 1987, during a conversation held a few days before he was murdered. In the course of that conversation Anaya pointed out a van with dark polarised windows which had drawn up outside. When the driver of the van noticed us peering through the Persian blinds he drew off. Anaya told us that this was a death squad car which came from the American embassy. His murder, like seventy thousand others in recent years may never be solved, because the judicial system of El Salvador (such as it is) falls beneath the control of the Armed Forces, and these are the assassins of thousands of defenceless people.

I'll always remember the words of Hérbert Anaya after witnessing the death squad van drawing away from the kerb. As we were taking leave of him one of the visiting priests accompanying us said, 'I wish you long life.'

Anaya shrugged his shoulders and answered, 'If I have a long life, then it would be more than thousands of my fellow patriots have been allowed to have.'

ROSES
August 1990

MIRTALA WAS ASTOUNDED AT the beautiful red roses growing freely in the gardens of Scotland. She said, 'When the war ends in El Salvador I'm going to plant roses everywhere.' She paused, 'No. When the war ends in El Salvador the first thing I'm going to do is build houses for my people, and then I'm going to plant roses everywhere. I'm also going to grow roses on the graves of my father and seven brothers and sisters killed by the Army . . . And if they kill me will you search for my grave and plant roses there?'

PREMATURE PARDON
30th September 1990

AT A PUBLIC MEETING in San Salvador three years ago, a priest was marvelling at the Salvadorean poor's capacity for forgiving the outrages committed against them. In an aside, young Tere remarked, 'Priests are always preaching pardon ...' She was rightfully annoyed at a passive, submissive, sweet, hollow understanding of what pardon means. In the last few weeks this important Christian concept has become clearer to my mind.

Arturo Rivera Damas, the Archbishop of San Salvador, is a wise old owl, a prudent preacher of the Word of God. Recently, feeling frustrated by the lies and cover-up perpetrated by the military personnel giving testimony in the case of the Jesuit priests murdered last November, he has been pressing for justice to be done and for all the material and intellectual authors of the crime to be brought to trial. This has irked certain members of Salvadorean society who tell the Archbishop, 'Stop asking for justice to be done in the case of the Jesuits. Forgive the assassins. Preach forgiveness, not justice.'

In reply, Archbishop Rivera quoted the Rector of the U.C.A., the Jesuit University. These were the words of Fr Francisco Estrada: 'Firstly, the truth. Then justice. And finally, forgiveness. In this order.'

This is borne out in the Gospel teaching. For example, in Jesus' parable about the king who forgave the servant who owed him ten million gold coins (Matthew 18:23-27), the king doesn't pardon the rogue immediately. Having established the *truth* of the situation (the servant's guilt), he sets about seeing that *justice* be done (sell the man, his wife and children into slavery). And only when there is an act of *repentance* from the guilty servant does the king show mercy and *pardon* him. But the man's repentance is insincere with no change in his callous behaviour. So, the king has justice carried out to the full, for there can be no pardon without real repentance.

Truth, justice, repentance and pardon (or amnesty, to use political language) is the correct human and Christian procedure in the case of the Jesuits and in every case of human rights abuse. Pardon should never precede truth, justice and sincere repentance.

THE TALE OF THE
WATER TAP
1st December 1990

WHAT THE EL HIGUERAL water tap whispered to me on the
1st of October 1988:

> 'I suppose you could call me a public servant. I'm
> always available, a permanent fixture jutting out from
> the side of the concrete water tank. Every day my top
> gets twisted to right and to left by young and old. I
> obey their wishes; twist me right and water gushes
> forth and the community is sustained, refreshed and
> cleansed by me. Twist me left and, hermetically, I hush
> into passive silence. Hands of all shapes, sizes and ages
> are lain on my brass top, so much so that my crown has
> become worn and shining like a bald head.

> 'Yesterday shook me up. In the afternoon a young
> guerrilla lad filled his water canister, turning my head
> right and left. The water gurgled and slurped, filling
> his green plastic water container to the brim. Mouth
> to mouth, the canister whispered that she had been
> part of the United States' government's military aid
> to the Salvadorean oligarchy and armed forces. With
> her brother, the M16 rifle, slung idly across her
> present master's shoulder, she had switched owners.
> This exchange occurred six years ago when the FMLN
> guerrilla laid siege to Paraíso barracks, entered it, and
> plundered all military equipment within. A heap of
> booty was extracted that day, booty still in circulation
> throughout rebel-controlled territory.

> 'In the evening, a few hours after my encounter
> with the guerrilla water canister, gunfire broke out
> in the hamlet. It rang out long and loud. Then there

fell a lull, a pregnant silence of some five minutes. Next, a hand turned my head right and I was mouth to mouth with a soldier's water canister. It looked identical to the guerrilla's canister. I gulped and spluttered. The canister whispered, 'Phew. That was a close one. Thought I was going to get riddled to death. Subversives ambushed us, you know . . . Wish the U.S. government had let me stay in Fort Bragg and not sent me along with a shipment of weapons and ammunition. El Salvador is a right hell-hole, believe you me . . . my master, and every other forced recruit or voluntary soldier, serves the interests of the United States government. And maybe someday he'll be killed defending these interests . . .'

'At this point the army water canister was pulled hastily from my mouth and sealed, lest she say too much. It's not advisable to go shooting off your mouth in El Salvador. Here, you can only speak safely in whispers. Even the corn has ears.'

THE MURDER OF A SON
19th December 1990, San Francisco Morazán

ABOUT CHRISTMAS TIME SEVERAL years ago in Scotland, I remember being called out to a house where on the previous night a young twenty-one-year-old girl had been murdered. My mind numbed, my thinking froze. I got to the car and realised I had left the car keys on my study desk. Having retrieved the keys, I turned to the car and realised I had forgotten my prayer ritual. Then, on reaching the car a third time, I decided to return to the presbytery for some other forgotten item. The truth of the matter was, I didn't want to enter such a cruel and terrifying situation. But enter I did.

Speechless I sat before the distraught, weeping mother. I had no words to soothe the woman's devastated soul or heal her broken heart. Her son, who had discovered the girl's dead body a few hours before, sat on the floor reading a newspaper. It didn't take a great feat of observation to recognise a psychopathic trait of a very sick mind. Unhappily, worst suspicions were confirmed and, shortly afterwards, Michael was convicted of his sister's murder.

The personal anguish of people can prove difficult to face. This evening, I got that numb feeling again as I walked out to the main square of the village to offer condolences to Don Jorge, one of our two bus drivers. His twenty-one-year-old son, Calin Bolaneros, had been arrested, beaten and killed by the security forces opposite the cattle market in Aguilares four days ago.

On Saturday evening, between six o'clock and half past six, Calin, accompanied by his wife and two children, was driving along the main road, travelling to officiate as best man at a wedding in San Salvador. At the side of the road he noticed there had been an accident involving a bus belonging to Farela, the bus company with which he worked. Thinking he could be of some assistance he stopped the car and got out. Then he saw four guards of the National Police beating up his friends and fellow employees. He asked them to stop hitting them. 'What right have you to interfere?' they asked, and proceeded to rain blows on Calin. He tried to defend himself, but there were too many of them. He was overpowered, handcuffed and led away. They hit him with their rifle butts. Then one of the guards pulled his army knife from its sheath and plunged it into Calin's left side. His principal heart artery was severed and he lay bleeding to death at the side of the road. The Salvadorean Green Cross appeared on the scene, but were unable to save his life.

'There is no greater love than this: to lay down your life for your friends.' (John 15:13)

This is true. But what do you do about the killers of the Good Samaritan?

Jorge's face looked ashen, his frame seemed stooped and shrunken, his eyes doleful. I gripped his hand and offered my regret.

'I've just got to resign myself to it,' said Jorge, wiping away a fallen teardrop from his cheek. 'It's the will of God.'

I answered, 'Evil acts can never be the will of God . . . Did you report the murder to the Human Rights Office?'

'No, my boss said he would see to that. I'll ask him tomorrow and, if not, I'll go myself and do it.' Jorge said the last few words with a certain resolve in his tone of voice.

'If it goes unreported, the soldiers responsible will go unpunished and have free licence to commit more murders,' I remarked.

There was an uneasy silence. The problem in El Salvador is that the military consider themselves an authority above the law and very seldom (almost never) are they prosecuted for human rights violations.

'They're beasts,' said Jorge. He compared the military security forces to beasts, the same image used by early Christians to describe their persecutors and murderers, the Roman soldiers:

'I saw arise from the sea a beast with seven heads and

seven horns, and on their heads were emblazoned inscriptions challenging God.' (Revelation 13:1)

'It must be a terrible grief for you, your wife, and all the family. We're remembering you in our prayers.'

'May God reward you for that,' said Jorge with a brave smile on his lips.

We shook hands and parted.

YOU'RE SWEET
25th December 1990

SIX-YEAR-OLD JACQUELINE is good gas. She likes to blether a bit, and is given to the giggles. One day she sat on the doorstep of her house like a queen on her throne and warned me to go canny passing her Gran's mare. 'She's a wild one with a big kick . . . My Aunt Gladis is in my house.'

When I asked if she meant Aunt Gladis, a wild one with a big kick, was in her house, she found this amusing and gave out a burst of giggles.

Yesterday, Christmas Eve, I wasn't surprised to see Jacqueline approach and sit down beside me on the presbytery step. It was festive time and the village children were playing 'Piñata'.

A hollow paper doll representing a funny chicken was filled with sweets and hung dangling from a rope which had been swung across the bough of the almond tree. One of the children was then blindfolded and given a stick to beat the chicken and spill the sweets from its tummy onto the eager, puerile faces below. Most of the time the little girl swiped thin air, because the chicken was levered heavenwards, frustratingly out of reach. In the scrimmage which was sure to ensue the tough wee boys looked set to snatch the prey from their dainty counterparts of the fairer sex. Notwithstanding this, I encouraged Jacqueline to go across, to wait and try her luck when the chicken exploded. She hesitated and, decided 'nothing ventured, nothing gained', and went to join the group of excited children.

I'd forgotten about her until five minutes later she returned carrying two sweets in the palm of her hand. I was surprised. 'You managed to get a couple of sweets?' I asked.

'Charo gave them to me,' she admitted. 'I'm going to give you half.'

I didn't want to take candy from the mouths of babes, so

I refused her offer, but Jacqueline insisted. She put one of the toffees in her dress pocket and repeated, 'I'll give you half.' Thereupon she proceeded to break the toffee in two with solemn, Eucharistic dignity, and gave me half. The other toffee, needless to say, remained wholly in her pocket.

Honey, you're sweet.

1991

GRIEF WORK
17th January 1991

NINE YEARS AGO, WHEN I worked in Scotland, a twelve-year-old girl belonging to the parish youth club died suddenly of an asthma attack. Louise's death was a shock to all of us, but I received the news with relative calm. After soaking for a while in a hot bath (perhaps '*regressus ad uterum*'?), I set off to celebrate the Eucharist at an outpost chapel. En route a dog scampered across the road near the front wheels of the car. I hit the brakes with a hard jerk and, in a stupor, found myself out of the car wanting to strangle the fugitive hound.

At the evening Eucharist something happened inside of me and I broke down and wept in public. The tears trickled steadily down my cheeks, and convulsive sobs broke through the words of the prayers. But in vain were efforts to control this emotional outburst.

Now, years later, a little bit wiser, I wonder why I felt the need to hide what is a natural, God-given expression of sorrow. I envy the Jews who know how to wail out their grief at the wall of Jerusalem. This seems a very healthy practice. And when Jesus wept tears of bereavement for his friend, Lazarus, no one said to him, 'Don't cry.' On seeing his tears, they remarked, 'It goes to show how fond he was of him.'

Last Sunday, Melbi's mother died. Melbi is a fifteen-year-old catechist. Tender of years and unable to cope with the situation, she wept out her desperate sense of pain and loss. But her oldest sister, Marta, publicly rebuked her for crying so much and fed her tranquilizers. Earlier I had told Melbi in a quiet chat that hers was a terrible ordeal to undergo and there is no need to stifle her grief.

At her mother's graveside Melbi wailed. And when she withdrew a little behind the mourners, I approached and tried to coax her to leave the scene behind. 'I don't want to go,' she said. A woman approached and spoke well-meaning words which made me cringe. 'Don't cry,' the woman said. 'We're all going to die.'

Finally, the heartbroken girl was helped along the pathway, through the cemetery exit, and towards life outside.

Why is it that we don't allow the bereaved a little time, a little space, in which to pour out their hurt without trying to dam their tears and forbid the expression of their grief?

THE RAVAGES OF WAR
4th February 1991

I STOOD BEMUSED AT the heartrending division civil war causes. It not only divides a nation, it can also divide communities and families. In a community meeting recently, Niña Carmen requested prayer for her four sons killed in war. The split was obvious. Manuel had been executed by the Guerrilla for spying. Matías had been killed while fighting in one of the Army's elite units against the Guerrilla. On the other side of the divide, Rafael and Reyes had fallen fighting for the Guerrilla against the Army.

As I reflected an explosion shook the air. The current from the blast blew up my trouser legs as a pall of dark grey conclave smoke arose soberly from between the trees, about four hundred yards away. A soldier of Atlacatl had stepped on a Guerrilla mine. This happened to be the third such detonation we had heard in the two days since the soldiers started to search the length and breadth of the wooded hillside. Someone mentioned that in the course of this military operation a soldier thought he had struck it lucky when they chanced upon a cache of powdered milk in tins. Unfortunately, the tins were wired to a booby trap and there was yet another explosion.

On leaving the zone aboard a lorry stacked with planks of wood, we passed a soldier lying at the side of the roadway in the shade. His wounded right foot had been dressed with a bandage. Judging from the part of the foot jutting out it seemed that his skin had been peeled off, leaving raw red bone. He lay there wearing a green tee-shirt and coffee-coloured underpants, being guarded by ten of his colleagues. They were awaiting a white army vehicle with a Red Cross emblem. This vehicle ferries the Army dead and wounded from the war zone. This was formerly done by air, but helicopters are practically grounded now for fear of the guerrillas' Sam 7 land-to-air missiles recently purchased.

The following morning, after the Sunday Eucharist in Dulce

Nombre de María had been celebrated, a catechist from one of the hamlets situated among the hills came down to say that two members of his community had been arrested by the elite soldiers of Atlacatl. Francisco Santamaría and Lolo Santos were being accused of collaborating with the guerrillas in purchasing a quantity of food supplies for them. The prisoners were being escorted from the hills towards Dulce Nombre de María. I felt my stomach muscles tighten and my teeth clench with apprehension. Superfluous to say, Atlacatl have a rank bad reputation regarding human rights. I didn't feel like a valiant shepherd eager to defend his vulnerable sheep from savaging wolves. I felt afraid. This battalion was responsible for executing six Jesuit priests and their two female helpers fourteen months ago. My gut reaction coaxed me to stay indoors, keep a low profile, and make do with a prayer. But conscience is not to be stilled so easily. I took a deep breath and, consoling myself with the thought that the worst anyone could do was to torture and kill me, I set out to look for the commanding officer. 'The Lord is the stronghold of my life, before whom shall I shrink?'

A soldier led the way to a middle-ranking officer who gave consent for me to be brought before the Captain. He met me on the staircase with a warm smile and handshake. 'God bless you, Father,' he said. I knew his public relations patter was artificial. I asked about the fifty-three-year-old Francisco and the forty-one-year-old Lolo. Perhaps genuinely, he claimed not to know anything about them. He handed me an identity document. It belonged to another man arrested the previous day, Gregorio Peraza. The Captain next held out a sheet of paper with a list of war names and two coded columns. He claimed this paper had been confiscated from Peraza. 'He was feeding thirty guerrillas,' the Captain asserted. I happened to recognise at a glance the name of Maclovio. I knew he had been wounded in another zone a while ago. Maybe he had returned or maybe the list was an old one not belonging to Gregorio Peraza. I held my counsel and asked them to keep me informed about the prisoners.

'Don't worry. They won't be beaten up or anything like

that. We only want to investigate. Tell the family and the people to keep calm.' There appeared a smile on his lips, but there was also a hard glint in his eyes. I could feel it. 'May God bless you, Father,' the Captain repeated his benediction with a strong handshake, his left hand placed on my right shoulder. I smiled and thanked him for hearing my appeal.

An hour later another officer and his bodyguard arrived at the presbytery door and informed me that the two prisoners had been remanded in custody at Paraíso barracks.

That night we gave bedding and a little hospitality to the wives of the prisoners and to a daughter. Lolo's wife is heavily pregnant. At first light the three women set out on their journey, seeking the assistance of the International Red Cross and the Church's Legal Aid Office in the town of Chalatenango. They were anxious that their loved ones should return home from captivity as soon as possible.

ON SCHOLASTIC CERTAINTIES
4th March 1991

One night
an angel appeared,
did dance a pirouette on a pin head,
and, in a whisper,
to me said:
'Thomas, Thomas,
doubting Thomas,
dost thou believe in the existence of God?'

Shaking sleep-befuddled wits,
wiping heavy slumber from eyelids,
and screwing courage
to the pine bed post,
I muttered 'Mister,
doubt is gift,
gift from God,
because only carrot-biting asses,
like thee,
don't doubt.
I consider myself not to be
a carrot-biting ass
like thee.'

GRAB THE BULL
BY THE TAIL
22nd February 1991

MY SLEEP THAT NIGHT was superficial and restless, and when I heard a thick, hard, tapping sound coming from behind the wardrobe, I switched on the lightbulb and arose to investigate. There, clinging to the wall, was a mother scorpion; her venomous hooked tail had been knocking against the wooden panel. The insect was speedily dispatched from time and space with the aid of a stick. A baby scorpion nearby was also killed, and I returned to bed.

I dreamt of a pretty, but fatale, woman with a pistol. This blonde James Bond heroine was threatening to blow out my brains. I tried to disarm her, but was unsuccessful in the attempt. Resignedly, I sighed, 'The sweet Rose of Israel has turned into a murderess.' Feeling powerless, I woke up and thus managed to break the spell of the nightmare.

I knew that this dream had been triggered by recent happenings in the repopulation of Teosinte. We had considered this place to be a model community, but now the enchantment had been dispelled by instances of fraud, drunkenness and marital infidelity. It seemed that these people who had suffered persecution and eight years of long exile in neighbouring Honduras, having lost family, friends and possessions through war, were now set on turning Teosinte into modern-day Corinth. Old Turrado, a theology professor in Spain, used to counsel that we should never absolutise anything human. Be this as it may, it hurts to discover the jewel, so joyfully clasped in the palm of your hand, is really only a chunk of granite rock.

Three nights after the dream, we celebrated the Eucharist in Teosinte, and rubbed a cross of ashes onto our foreheads. Wake up and 'take another direction' was Jesus' Gospel message. We applied this to community life in the three areas of mismanagement of funds, drunken behaviour (which had resulted in two cases of wife-beating) and sexual infidelity.

Two brothers had bought twelve cows as their private property. One of these belonged to the community's group of directors. Cleverly they had grouped their cows with the community's, thus enjoying the benefits of injections, vaccinations, flour and other communal benefits attained by project money sent from Scotland. I pointed out that the project money was for the purchase and maintenance of co-operative cows, not capitalist ones. Although private property is not illegitimate if earned by the sweat of your brow, public money should not be used to maintain private property.

Speaking of drunkenness within the community, I told them that five parishioners, in less than four years, had died as a result of too much alcohol. Excessive intake of alcohol harms personal health, destroying the liver. It wastes money, which in poverty-stricken homes could be used for a family's nourishment and welfare. A far greater miracle than changing water into wine would be to change firewater into food. The bad example a drunken father gives to his children is detrimental to family upbringing and the moral development of a community. Drunks are nuisances and can become dangerously violent nuisances. They are also inconsistent in labour, missing work days through their over-indulgence.

The third area discussed was sexual infidelity. The Church's teaching proclaims marriage as one man and one woman in an exclusive communion of life and love until death should separate them. This is the necessary Gospel ideal to strive after and is the only secure foundation for family life. A constant pattern in this community was one man with more than one woman.

In the shadows, near the church door, members of the Guerrilla lurked, listening to what was being said. And later, in the darkness of night, Serafín the cattle-owner and three of his companions came to complain over the first point of the homily. I listened and asked for strict accounts in future regarding the cattle project funded by the Catholic Church in Scotland. But I don't believe they're behaving honestly. They were self-contradictory in certain statements they made. Serafín also claimed I was creating division in the community. I corrected him by stating that the wall was already cracked, gesturing at the split room wall behind them. 'You created the division by bringing about material inequality through private ownership on a big scale. I was only stating the obvious.'

They were unable to counter this and sank into silence. It is an unfortunate fact of life that you have got to break eggs to make omelettes.

THINGS BRIGHT
AND BEAUTIFUL
21st April 1991

FREQUENTLY, WHEN I SIT eating tortillas and frijol beans in the corridor of a house, the kitchen cat miaows, rears on her hindquarters and punches beseechingly at my knees for a share of the fare. There are three ways of responding to this feline supplication. First way: try to ignore the little lady. But this is not so easy when she has the nasty tendency to sink her claws into your kneecaps. Second way: try to get her to depart. Gently fend Miss Kittie from the table radius with your feet. Unfortunately, this is not practical, because it means employing an incessant Stanley Matthews' shuffle with the ginger ball of fur throughout the prolongation of the meal. And so, the third option: yield and share a little of the plate's contents.

Having recently read Paul Gallico's fascinating tale of the cat world, *Jennie*, I was more disposed than usual to break off a chunk of maize pancake and share with my feline companion. But, at the very moment of breaking tortilla with the cat, Niña Santos produced a fourth, and most effective, solution: a bucketful of water cascaded through the air as Zapi scuttled to safety through the gate's spars, her coat bristling with H_2O. She kept her distance for the duration of the meal.

One night, while sleeping in the log cabin of Yerba Buena, I heard a grating sound in the darkness outside. I checked my watch – ten minutes to two. What on earth could be the cause of this sinister noise? I waited, hoping the crunching sound would stop, but it seemed to increase in volume and intensity. Imaginings came to mind. Had the dogs uncovered the bones of the three guerrillas killed in combat and buried in Yerba Buena during the past five years? I thought this the likeliest explanation.

Stealthily, I crept from bed and poked my head out of the doorway. A few yards' distance stood a mule crunching its molars into a bone-dry water dish. The beast was thirsty and craved water. I fetched a basin and filled the dry, hollow stone which served as a water dish. And the sound changed to the lapping of water.

On the afternoon of Good Friday the people of San Fernando Antiguo were moving in silent procession with the statue of the crucified Christ in order to commit it to symbolic burial in a house across the river. It was a solemn procession, almost lugubrious in tenor. We crossed the narrow, wooden bridge without a handrail. The water rushed and gushed white foam ten feet beneath the spars, reminiscent of a rabid dog's jaws. Suddenly, a splash was heard and a titter of amusement rippled through the air. My immediate thought was that someone had slipped and fallen but, as it happened, a youngster had edged over the side a mongrel hound which pulled itself unhappily from the water, trailing an injured hind leg behind. I felt sorry for the dumb beast, butt of human cruelty.

The stench of death reeked through the air. It seemed to emanate from the top corner of the house, inside the rafters. Owing to infestation we had placed rat poison on the floor and I suspected a dead rat was rotting above. A battalion of ants scuffling to and fro confirmed this suspicion.

With the aid of a stepladder I climbed to the spot, inhaling putrid air and involuntarily turning my face to the side, but was unable to reach the spot because the roof tiles hemmed it in. Pedro, the Celebrator of the Word, ascended the ladder, but the waft of death forced him to beat a retreat.

Putting on a surgical mask soaked in alcohol Pedro advanced once more, removed a couple of tiles and extracted from the corner a light brown, decapitated rat. Ants had eaten its entire head. He flung the carcass to the ground and I dumped it further afield.

That night, another light brown rat pattered across the rafter directly above my bed. On relaying this information to Pedro next morning, he sighed, 'What a shame. It's searching for its missing partner.'

Heartfelt compassion, even for the animal world, is a gift Pedro possesses in profusion. His spirit mirrors the gentleness of St Francis. In his personal life, he has had to endure the harrowing loss of his wife, whose untimely accidental death ten years ago has left a melancholic strain in his soul, despite a cheery demeanour. Add to this the loss of his young son who died fighting for the Guerrilla, and the loss of two brothers who were sacrificed for the same cause, and the suffering of Pedro can be imagined. He has had a rough row to hoe, and perhaps he was seeing his own sense of loss and bewilderment reflected in the loss and bewilderment of a grieving rat.

THE MOTHER CHILD
15th June 1991

Ofelia is
nine years, not old,
yet she has a woman's face, not a child's;
adult cares have etched out
agedness four decades before her time.
She smiles a solemn Mona Lisa smile,
but brown eyes, mirroring her soul, bulge
like a frightened, wounded doe's.

Each day of drudgery
Ofelia's scarecrow stick-bone arms cradle
the burden of an infant brother
until night's reprieve bids settle upon her repose,
and the oblivion of sleep.

Ofelia is
another mother child
precipitated by poverty
into immature maternity.

A LEAP IN THE DARK
3rd August 1991

Hear the lies,
see the sin,
smell the shit,
touch powerlessness,
feel anger,
weep tears,
and commit yourself to life
or to death.

A LESSON TOO LATE
30th August 1991, San Francisco Morazán

MUST DO THE SHOPPING, I thought. Forthwith I flicked off my rubber flip-flop house footwear and picked up a right Reebok training shoe and sank naked foot into it. My big toe knocked against something and I hesitated that critical split second, imagining a cockroach or a grasshopper. Then pain flashed with poisonous velocity from toe to brain and I pulled out my stung foot and cradled it in my hands, issuing a war cry which made Fred Flintstone's 'Yabba-Dabba-Doo' sound like a primeval whimper.

The black scorpion, preened to full length, dashed from the fallen shoe to safety, slipping under the door of Henry's bedroom. There, in sanctuary, I suspect she nestles snug behind an over-stacked bookshelf, and I would be loath to remove this precarious piece of furniture for fear of couping everything to the floor. Hopping to the fridge I quaffed a few glasses of Cola. My thoughts raced along in panic: ingest sugar into bloodstream; pack foot with ice; suck sweets; take aspirins; take hot tea. I resisted the lure of Johnnie Walker. Dull, aching spasms went shooting through my body, and my right hand felt weak and wobbly as I tried to finish off a letter. At an early hour of the following morning my tongue tingled, although the pain of the scorpion venom had long since departed.

In future, I resolve to shake my shoes before putting them on, and so avoid further mishaps of a similar nature.

THE ARMY
DEATH SQUADS
29th September 1991

MR IAN MURRAY, THE British Consulate in El Salvador, recently told a colleague of mine that 'there is an average of only three Death Squad killings a month in El Salvador'.

Some of us believe that this is an average of three too many, and that there can be no complacent acceptance of terror carried out by El Salvador's military.

Five days ago, I visited a friend, Mirtala López, a director of the Christian Commission for Displaced People. That morning she had received her fourth typed death threat from 'The Salvadorean Anti-Communist Front' in twelve days. The following are extracts taken from the four letters.

9 September We eliminated the Jesuits of the U.C.A. Just so, we are firm in our resolve to terminate the lives of those who profess to be leaders of Machiavellian guerrilla organizations ... YOUR YOUTH IS ON THE BRINK OF DANGER. YOUR END IS DRAWING NEAR.

18 September We have SWORN not to fail: we intend to cut the heads off terrorist leaders. The blood of those who act against democracy is required in order to bring peace and tranquillity to the nation. YOUR YOUTH IS TO BE BROUGHT TO AN END TODAY.

21 September Your movements are being strictly monitored by our heroic FRONT and they have strict orders to end your life: *WE WANT YOUR HEAD.* The United Nations Corps in El Salvador is no safeguard for you, because they too are our enemies. Stop at once your defamatory campaigns against our front. All they do is hasten the end of your LITTLE HEAD MIRTALA LÓPEZ.

24 September Do not flee, our weapons are upon YOUR BODY; THEY WILL TASTE THE BLOOD GUSHED FROM YOUR VEINS. *WE ARE CERTAINLY GOING TO CARRY THIS OUT.*

'To live is to participate in the struggle [for a just society]; to participate in the struggle [for a just society] is to live,' Mirtala explained.

'Survive and participate in the struggle,' I urged her. 'Go into hiding.'

She told me that she was leaving the office in ten minutes, having been offered asylum in a European embassy in the city. From there she would seek an entrance visa for the United States.

I felt relieved. For her to stay would mean certain death at the hands of callous, cowardly men who menace and murder defenceless women.

We embraced and parted.

THE FLIGHT OF A CAPTIVE BIRD
10th November 1991

MARTA PASSED AWAY AT four o'clock in the morning. Thirty years old, her body had become a twisted burden, her teeth protruded, her eyes declared the mind absent, and her tongue was incapable of words, only sounds could she utter.

Day after day she would sit on the dirt floor of her house, lost in a world of oblivion, while the tiny Niña Chus, Marta's mother, attended her only child's needs with silent heroism and dedication. I never cease to be amazed at the love, sheer willpower and painstaking effort of a mother who serves her handicapped child. Such people evangelise us, revealing in practice the real depth and meaning of the word 'love'.

Their house stands at the exit of the village and I made a habit of saying 'Hello' to Marta each time I passed on the road to the northern communities of the parish. Always she would guffaw with laughter and try to hide her face. But I would persist with my salutation, joining in the fun. When I remember Marta I'll always remember her laughing. Maybe it was the beard, maybe it was the foreign accent but, unfailingly, she would let out a burst of hilarity when I looked at her and spoke.

She was a useful member of the community although she could do no work. In a sense Marta was our teacher, although she could neither speak, nor read, nor write. She taught us gentle innocence and unforced laughter. She taught us the humility to accept the unchangeable limits imposed by our conditions and circumstances, to accept vulnerability and failure. The lessons derived from Marta's stay among us we may never fully comprehend.

At the cemetery I cringed on discovering that the gravediggers had been drinking the local firewater and were a bit worse for wear. My fears seemed well-founded when a rope slipped as the coffin was being lowered to the bottom of the grave. The hollow thud of the corpse banging against the wood caused Niña Chus to wail and weep aloud. I tried to comfort her. 'People scorned my daughter,' she told me between sobs. Later, on leaving the cemetery, one of the 'Knights of the Holy Sepulchre', carrying his spade on a shoulder as if it were a rifle, shrugged and muttered, 'It doesn't really matter if they go down gently or with a crash; the dead don't feel anything anyway.'

Once the coffin had been rearranged the drunk gravediggers filled in the grave of Marta. One of them wiped his brow and dug the spade into a neighbouring grave. 'Is this yours?' he asked a woman mourner.

'No,' she answered nervously in front of everyone. 'That's my piece over there. I'll be buried in that place.'

In fact, he wanted to know if the spade belonged to her.

Sometimes, in life, tragedy unfolds like a pantomime.

I also noticed that two of our discarded Plumrose sausage tins had been picked up from the village rubbish tip and placed on the cement table slab of a grave. These tins now served as flower vases. This made me smile. From now onwards, on opening a tin of Plumrose sausages, I'll remember the dead. 'Memento mori.'

INCEST
November 1991

ROSA, A TEN-YEAR-OLD girl, said to me, 'My Mum wants to speak to you?'

Later that day I climbed the slope towards her house. Suddenly, as I reached the entrance, a brown dog sprang towards me, teeth bared, snarling and barking. The brute made a few attempts at sinking its incisors into the marrow of my shinbone, but I managed to stave it off with some nifty footwork. The animal seemed to be possessed, reminiscent of the hound in the horror movie *The Omen*.

Finally, after what seemed like an eternity, the woman I intended to visit stepped from the shadows of her house and called the dog off. It slackened and I picked up a heavy stone to make it beat a speedy retreat through the cornfield.

The adrenalin pumped through my arteries. The mother of Rosa approached and explained that the dog belonged to her husband's brother-in-law who lived over a mile away. Often it arrived at their house because it was unhappy in the brother-in-law's place.

I knew the brother-in-law only too well. A decade ago he was an active member of the village death squad. Recently, I had confronted him publicly regarding his allegiance to a protestant sect and made it plain I accepted his decision to join them, although I would strike his children's names off the parish baptismal register for his apostasy. In retrospect, it would probably have been wiser to be grateful that such as he was no longer a Catholic. The blood of the poor spilt by this man and his companions cries aloud to the heavens.

That same evening Pérez stalked the village like a wild and wounded lion. Carrying a sharp, two-foot agricultural blade he blustered that he was out to get Padre Tomás. But, not coincidentally, to allow tension to cool a little, I had left to visit a neighbouring community earlier in the day.

Owner and dog, two of a kind, I thought; both rabies-ridden.

'The dog's owner is a bad one,' I told the woman. 'He beats his wife and kids. A cruel man.'

She nodded assent. 'My husband does the same to me. I've got to leave this place. Can you help me? He hits me hard when he gets drunk, and once tried to rape Rosa, our daughter.'

At this point in the conversation the man in question appeared from the side of the house, 'Why didn't you call the dog off? You were only a few yards away,' asked his wife.

He made no response and walked sullenly indoors, head down.

I beckoned the woman aside and asked permission to question him regarding his behaviour. She assented.

Feeling in no mood for applying Carl Rogers' accurate empathy counselling technique, I decided to 'bowl fast for the middle stump'. Looking glacially into his eyes I voiced a blatant threat: 'You lay one cowardly finger of assault on your wife again, and I'll make sure the men of this community chastise you physically and expel you from here. And if I hear you even attempt to have sexual intercourse with your young daughter, I'll make it a personal crusade to take you to the tribunals and get you put behind bars for many years to come. Be warned. If your behaviour doesn't improve we'll take strong action against you.'

This was the fourth case of incestuous rape or attempted incestuous rape known in the parish during these last five years. It's a perplexing, horrendous reality and I suspect it happens to a lot more womenfolk than we would ever imagine.

THE NIGHTMARE
14th December 1991

FRANCISCO, THE GUERRILLA DOCTOR, related a highly significant experience of the unconscious world which happened when his platoon was stationed in San Juan, Portillo.

He saw himself seated in the back of a train carriage careering along in the darkness of the night. Outside was blackness and threat. All of a sudden, ghoulish faces with fearsome eyes gazed at him through the window glass. Francisco felt frightened. A voice called out, 'Dad!' And he awoke from the nightmare startled.

It was three o'clock in the morning. The doctor was to remember those few moments in August, because later he was to receive word that, simultaneous to that nightmare, his twenty-year-old son was flung from a five-storey flat to his death. The murder of his favourite child in Mexico at the hands of a death squad was registered in the unconscious mind of Francisco on the day and hour of the occurrence.

'I feel hate for the killers. My son was doing political work for us at the time. Well do I understand the compulsion to kill of these youngsters in our ranks whose loved ones have been murdered by the soldiers. That feeling of revenge is gut-deep ... I thought of taking up the rifle and going on a mission to kill soldiers, but decided to transform this useless feeling of hate into healing, promoting and organising the good of the people. That's the best revenge.'

'I'm telling you of this experience so that you can file it away in your library,' added Francisco, with a smile of sadness.

THE CROSS AND THE EARTHLY BANNER

20th December 1991

HIGH ON A HILL overlooking Valle de Jesús arises from the earth a wooden cross. Recently a red FMLN guerrilla flag was draped across it. This made me feel uncomfortable, so I resolved to climb the hill and take down the flag, carry it to the village square, and tie it beneath another red flag flying from a bamboo plant.

Too often nations and political groups (including the Church) have exploited the true meaning of the cross, making it serve as justification for behaviour opposed to the Spirit of Christ. But the cross must stand alone and judge all creeds and all political thinking in every age. The Carpenter, tortured and executed by the powerful, is the vindication of the crucified victims of history, whoever and wherever they may be.

As I descended the path between the rocks thoughts churned in my mind. I thought, no war should ever be described as being 'just', because the word 'justice' is a sacred word evoking fullness of life; it should never be applied adjectively to killing – regardless of the underlying motive for dealing death. The term 'just war' is contradictory – not paradoxical. Pace Thomas Aquinas.

Neither can war rightly be called 'holy'. War is never the will of God. It's always the result of man's greed and cruelty on a large scale. Those who crusade and kill 'in the name of God' are deceiving themselves, for God is the God of life.

However, at times, war can be a necessary last resort in order to defend the poor against unremitting tyranny. Yet such a revolutionary war, as that of El Salvador, should only be accepted with ambivalence (never absolutising violence) and conditioning it to historical change, which means that, ultimately a revolution should bring more good than harm.

My mind's churning ended with the words of Sergio Méndez, that wise old Bishop of Cuernavaca in Mexico: 'Entre fe y revolución no hay contradicción. Pero tampoco hay identificación.' 'Between faith and revolution there lies no contradiction. But neither can the two be considered the same thing.'

SOMOS UNA SOMBRA
27th December 1991

LAST NIGHT I DREAMED a dream of loss. Two golden teeth had fallen from my mouth, and I knew that these golden teeth somehow belonged to me. This imagery was followed by the frightened squawking sound of two white seagulls gliding through the sky. A feeling of anguish gripped my soul.

As I write, the words of old, deaf Teresa come to mind. She described to me the passing of her ancient mother in a platonic vein: 'Somos una sombra'. 'We are but a shadow. A shadow.'

I remember recently handing over to Niña Dulia the birth certificate of her child, dated 1979. This certificate had been discovered during a spring cleaning of the parish archives. Standing in the corridor of her one-room house she looked at me sadly and said, 'Santos is dead. He died on the day government soldiers invaded El Higueral, the 14 February 1981. You know, we didn't even have time to pray a wake over him. We had to flee our homes and leave everything behind. Purificación dug the child's grave with a scythe in Isotalillo.'

As I listened to her words I thought how the pain of a persecuted people is deep and perennial. Last month, in another community, I paid a visit to the house of Lidia and asked for a tortilla to eat since I felt hungry. With customary graciousness she attended to my request. We got talking about a community cow that had died while giving birth. In the background blood-red, chunky slices of meat hung from the roof's rafters and flies swarmed around. This was the family's portion of the fare. I remembered the dead pig's head speared on top of a sharpened stick in William Golding's classical novel, *The Lord of the Flies*.

'The calf wouldn't budge anymore; only half of it was able to slide out of the mother cow's womb,' Lidia said. 'Four men tugging were unable to deliver it and it died stillborn. Dogs ate its half-born corpse . . . Dogs ate my father's corpse too.'

She expressed this horrific fact without melodrama. It was simply a statement of fact; dogs had eaten her father's corpse.

Lidia continued, 'Twenty-three people died that day in El Roble, a hamlet of Chalatenango, including a pregnant woman who was ill in bed when the soldiers came. All those who decided to stay in their homes rather than take flight with us into the nearby hills were lined up against a wall and shot without mercy. Men, woman and children were killed. Their remains were left unburied, given over as food for the dogs and vultures. We couldn't return to bury them until it was safe. It was my Uncle Rudolfo who buried the pieces of his brother, my father.'

The sorrow and travail of the Salvadorean people crucified violently by an omnipotent army should never be ignored, or forgotten, so long as the sands of time run. An end to these oppressive military structures is demanded, because the poor of El Salvador have substance. They are of infinite value. They are not a mere shadow.

1992

THE UNFINISHED
SYMPHONY
16th January 1992

'Of the dark past, a child is born:
With joy and grief my heart is torn.'

James Joyce

THRONGS OF PEOPLE CRUSHED into the square opposite
the cathedral in San Salvador to celebrate the signing of the
peace accord between the Salvadorean government and the
FMLN guerrilla. The sixteenth of January, nineteen hundred
and ninety two, will be remembered in history as the signing
of the peace document in Mexico which brings to a formal end
twelve years of bloodshed in El Salvador. I stood and watched
as members of the FMLN unravelled a huge national flag to
the right of the national palace. To the left they unravelled
an equally large red rebel flag. The atmosphere tingled, and
thunderous applause filled the skies. It was a privilege to be
there, witnessing the clandestine coming to light. And in the
cathedral bell tower Radio Venceremos, the Guerrilla radio,
emitted over the air its first legal transmission.

Life buzzed all around, but two images gave food for
thought. The first was that of a middle-aged man waving
a small United States flag, and another younger man, with
the fire brandishing in his eyes, protesting this action. I
understood the anger of the young man: the government of
the United States invested 6 billion dollars during the eighties
promoting and fomenting El Salvador's civil war.

Then I saw the quasi-apocalyptic image of an old woman, face
worn and etched by suffering, resolutely holding a small wooden
cross with Archbishop Romero's photo pinned to it. There she
stood, a powerful symbol of the poor in the same square where

people were killed by sniper bullets and crushed to death by the ensuing panic during the funeral Mass of the Archbishop. And I heard in my heart the words Romero addressed in the letter to President Carter on the 17th of February 1980.

'Sending military equipment and assessors will, beyond doubt, heighten the injustice and repression against this politically organised people who have struggled and struggled for their most basic human rights to be respected.

'Forbid that this military assistance be given to the government of El Salvador.

'Do not intervene. The people are preparing themselves to be the responsible agent of El Salvador's future. Only they are able to overcome this crisis.

'It would be unjust and intolerable that foreign powers meddle and frustrate the Salvadorean people, repressing them, preventing them from deciding for themselves the political and economic plan which our homeland should put into practice.

'Accept my request and so avoid a greater spilling of blood in this suffering country.'

His call went unheeded. Five weeks later, they murdered the prophet Romero as he celebrated the Eucharist.

There was a minute of applause (not silence) dedicated to those who shed their lifeblood for the liberation of the people. The applause was but for a minute, yet our thanks to those who died defending the poor from the oppressor should be eternal.

NOT ME, MY DEAR
20th April 1992

I SAT IDLY ON the steps of the threshold of the church and watched the world go by. Eight-year-old Cristina stopped in front of me with stars in her eyes, sighed, and said, 'Padre, you look like the Lord.'

Left speechless, I smiled and reminded myself to go for a haircut at the earliest opportunity.

THE CASTING OF THE CURSE
April 1992

THE SQUAT, SOLEMN, BROODING Pilgrim Lady was one of the community's statues removed from the church of Tremedal when the villagers fled the army repression eleven years ago. Eufemia kept this statue in her house of exile and refused to part with it when a sector of the original population repopulated their place of origin. And, without consultation, she sold the image to the nearby community of Ojos de Agua for forty pesos.

In the course of time the people living in Tremedal discovered that their treasured community symbol had been sold and made efforts to recover it. But to no avail. So they asked for my intercession. Being a clandestine iconoclast I hesitated. Then I decided, with a shade of reluctance, to write a letter requesting the return of 'La Peregrina' to her rightful abode. This appeal went unheeded.

Some weeks later, while conversing with someone from Ojos de Agua I happened to mention that there would befall a curse upon the entire community should they persist in their refusal to surrender the stolen Virgin.

Word got round and the contact from Ojos de Agua returned to San Francisco to remonstrate with me, 'We haven't got the statue. You can go and search every house if you like.'

'I know you haven't got it,' I replied, 'It was given back last week. Thank you.'

'And the curse?' he asked.

'Blessings and salutations be upon the community of Ojos de Agua,' I quipped with a wry smile.

DEMOBILISED
23rd September 1992

I WAS A LITTLE surprised to see Rosa step down from the lorry and come towards me. The last time I remembered seeing her she was sitting in silence, patiently sewing a coloured thread design on a white, bleached flour bag. Today she looked different in her green, black-spotted trousers and green guerrilla tee-shirt. Her mood was different too. She wasn't subdued; she breezed cheerfulness.

'When are you heading for Valle de Jesús?' she asked, perhaps feeling a little insecure walking in war togs through a community which had never given full adherence to the revolution. Rosa had belonged to the latest contingent of ex-guerrillas who were returning to civilian life after temporary concentration under the supervision of the United Nations.

The following morning she arrived forty-five minutes late, having journeyed on foot from Jocote where she had lodged the night. Although a permanent ceasefire was in operation and the war had ended, I felt rather uncomfortable walking openly through San Juan de la Cruz. The roadworkers stopped to stare at their priest escorting a pretty young lady along the dirt track. Robin Hood and Maid Marion hit the road, I mused. Lucio and Juana, whose soldier son was killed in a guerrilla ambush a decade ago, waved in salutation and feigned a smile, but their eyes seemed cold and angry. I can understand their annoyance.

Rosa's step had spring in it, possibly a result of her too-tight white training boots, which were a demobilisation gift from the FMLN along with a Japanese Walkman whose wires hung from her neck like a necklace.

I remember having baptised her first child, Margarito, who bore the war name of his guerrilla father. And seven days after giving birth to their second child Rosa received news that Margarito, her husband, had been killed in battle. Rosa's brother, Sego, also fell in battle about the same time.

'The war was hard on you.'

'Yes,' she replied, 'but what happened to me made me even more determined to go on in the struggle.'

We got to talking about the plight of the widows in the community and she told me that Marina and Ricarda had been admonished by the FMLN for selling firewater. Marina was made to work in the nursery while only God knows to where they assigned Ricarda. We remembered how Ricarda used to get tiddly on the local hooch and wreak havoc among the other women, like an angry cat among docile pigeons. The nursery children learned new vocabulary in these frequent bouts. Sometimes life's tragedies bear a little hidden humour.

'Ricarda's pregnant again,' declared Rosa.

'Like the Virgin Mary,' I remarked. She laughed aloud, and I wished I could have swallowed back my words. Maybe comparing Mary, the single-parent mother from rural Nazareth, with Ricarda, the merry war widow from Valle de Jesús, was not a joke in good taste. Ricarda, after all, had had more men than the woman at the well.

'Who's the father?' I asked gullibly. Rosa shrugged her shoulders.

'Ah well,' I continued, 'so long as she doesn't blame St Joseph.' Rosa's laughter pealed out again. Then she made a sad statement of fact: 'All the widows in Valle de Jesús have got pregnant after their men died fighting for the Guerrilla. All except me, that is.'

She laughed again. It was a child's laugh. Like the child at play who boasts to her companion:

> 'Ha, ha, ha
> hee, hee hee,
> the stinging, buzzing bumble bee
> couldn't catch me.'

And the truth of Rosa's words sank in. Bereavement, a sense of lasting loss, a natural sex-drive pertinent to most human beings, and a great insecurity regarding their future material existence, has driven these women into shallow, transient sexual encounters with unplanned, unwanted offspring resulting. The consequences of war are sadder than we dare imagine.

A CRIPPLED OLD MAN
8th October 1992

'If a madman drives his car along the pavement, as
a pastor, I just can't bury the dead and comfort the
bereaved. I have to tear the driver away from the
wheel.'

Dietrich Bonhoeffer

I SAT ON ONE of the front seats of the bus and idly gazed
through the rectangular window frame at the front of the bus.
The mundane scenery of Salvadorean city life portrayed street
vendors, flow of traffic, and the bustle and swarm of the people.
But in a matter of a few seconds this platonic cinema screen
before me showed a scene of surrealistic horror. An old man
on crutches fell beneath the wheels of a Mercedes Benz van
reversing at high speed. He writhed, twisted, and screamed as
the back right wheel passed over his already crippled legs. His
crutch snapped in two pieces like brittle bone, and the front right
wheel bumped over his legs. I gasped and watched the van career
towards our bus.

'¡Cuidado!' 'Watch out!' I shouted, a second before the
vehicle smashed into the front of our cruising bus. Yorlando,
the driver, hit the brakes hard. I had braced myself with arms
shielding eyes and face from possible broken glass. Our bus
jerked to a halt. Muttering an expletive in English, I leapt onto
the road and ran towards the crippled old man lying near the
kerb. The long, cream-coloured van of dark polarized windows
and drawn curtains had cut a diagonal path across the road and
smashed against a new, blue pick-up parked opposite, breaking
off his vehicle's bumper before grinding to a halt.

We had been fortunate. A second later it would have hit us
full on, with possible fatal consequences. Instead it had hit our
front bumper and ricocheted away.

The old man groaned, fear and fright in his eyes. I knelt down at his side and propped up his head from the hard, tarmac road, smoothing his thin, grey hair with my hand, trying to comfort him as best I could. He told me his right leg had no feeling in it and the left was much the same.

Laying his head down gently I went to a shop and bought a large towel. When I came out, they had lifted the victim onto the back compartment of a white pick-up. I placed the towel under his head and they drove off.

Feeling anger well up inside of me I walked to the other side of the road where a national policeman stood, taking details.

'I'll pay for everything,' said the plump lady in a purple dress outfit.

'Human life has no price,' I remarked acidly.

'There was someone knocked down,' declared the policeman.

I added, 'I'm prepared to go to the courts of law as a witness. I saw everything from the front seat of the bus, and you were responsible.' I nodded in her direction. 'I'm not afraid to speak the truth as an eye-witness and as a Catholic priest.'

At this, the woman driver's sagging breasts sagged further, her eyes closed, and her head bowed in silent submission. She was well and truly 'cooked', as the Salvadoreans would say. She had no licence and her daughter had been giving Mummy an improvised driving lesson. I jotted down my name and address on the back of the policeman's pad, as requested, and he shook my hand, thanking me profusely for my spirit of co-operation.

Five minutes later, escorted by two armed national police, the daughter got behind the wheel to drive the Mercedes Benz van to the police pound for confiscation. I reminded her a little bluntly that the knocked-down cripple was due compensation and the payment of his hospital bills. She never replied verbally, but shot me a frozen glance. I stepped back and watched the vehicle pull out.

Three hours afterwards, Mummy Learner (looking as glum as a cooked goose), accompanied by her daughter, boarded our bus to visit a garage and receive an estimate of the bus's repair. She had gone to the hospital to square medical damages and pay compensation to the old man's relatives. Mummy belittled the cripple's injuries. 'No serious fractures,' she said. 'A bang on the hip bone and a scrape on the head.' I had seen him knocked around like a rag doll, so I reminded her that two wheels of her van had crushed a prostrate victim's legs and that only she was to blame for what had happened.

She answered, 'He's a drunk. He spends his time begging about here. He was so filthy the nurse had to give him a wash . . .'

'He's a human being,' I reminded her.

A PARTING GIFT
18th October 1992

THE FLU BUG LEFT me feeling faint so, after celebrating the Eucharist, I entered the small room attached to the church, closed the door, and lay down on the canvas bed to rest.

A few moments later a disembodied voice said, 'It's locked.' Sniffling I arose to open the door. The daylight flooded in and the glare hurt my eyes. Like a nun of an unknown order, her unchanged headscarf tied tightly round her head, her brown-framed glasses with the left stem missing askew on the bridge of her nose, there before me stood Niña Magdalena. She handed over an offering of two blobs of cold fried banana on a tin plate, and a grubby plastic bag containing a slab of orange cake. Throughout six years I've found this woman's simple kindness very moving and, on that occasion, I expressed sincere thanks, using the customary formula, 'Qué Dios se lo pague.' 'May God pay you for this.'

'When are you coming back to visit?' chirped the wiry little bird.

'I've pinned a paper with details on the church door,' I told her, not remembering the date of my next visit to the community. Calendar dates don't mean too much to people who cannot read or write and who have little sense of time and punctuality. Niña Magdalena had come very late for Mass that afternoon, and after the celebration was over she approached to ask a special, private blessing for the bowl of water she had brought, having arrived too late to participate in the communal blessing at the start of Mass. The belief is that blessed water will ward off evil spirits.

'Why do you want to know when I'll return?' I enquired.

'I might not be here,' she answered cryptically.

'Where are you going to?'

She never answered this question with words. Instead, she raised her brown eyes heavenwards and made an Indian-like gesture of a bird taking wing from the palm of her hand.

I found this puzzling. She seemed to be in spanking good health. 'Come now, Niña Magdalena, you'll be around for a long, long time.'

She looked at me dubiously.

When we parted with a handshake I gazed at the offerings and decided to chance eating the sweetbread, putting it for safe-keeping in a clean plastic bag. I then cut the yellow watery banana with a spoon and raised it slowly to my lips. I stopped halfway and returned the gift of the poor to the plate. Walking through the doorway I cast a furtive glance around the corner in the direction of Niña Magdalena's house. The coast was clear. No human being was in sight; only Gloria's chickens and her lean, downcast dog tied to the fence post. I almost tiptoed towards my canine companion and scooped the bananas onto the hard soil. With frantic slurps he gobbled the sweet fare.

I looked around me once more; the guilty child within wanted to ensure I hadn't been caught out. No human presence. Only some chickens, a dog, and God.

Three weeks later Niña Magdalena died. Just as she said she would.

The day of her death she had risen from bed and prayed the rosary beads, like a Buddhist monk reciting his repetitive mantra. Repeatedly, Mary, the mother of Jesus, was beseeched: 'Pray for us sinners now, and at the hour of our death.'

After prayer she asked her son-in-law to climb the orange tree and shake down some ripe oranges. He climbed and Magdalena sang a hymn, slowly stooping to pick up the fruit fallen from above. Singing a sacred song, in simple communion with creation, in the early morning light, an old woman's soul parted this world and soared heavenwards. It was as if an eager, sprightly bird had sprung from an open palm, giving a deft farewell touch before commencing the long journey home.

1993

A DREAM INVITING
REGENERATION
9th February 1993

IT IS NIGHT-TIME and I know I must cross the courtyard to reach that red Blairs staircase. This particular seminary staircase is a place which curtails expression. Speech is not allowed there. It also leads to the classrooms where we ingest new, scientific knowledge. More mental toil, more input, more study. Life is a serious, rational business.

But the dark courtyard below is filled with playful, mischievous, free, spontaneous monkeys. Their unconscious selves are given loose rein; no one hampers their expression. I walk amidst the morass of moving, merry creatures, and one of them jumps up and taps me on the back of the head reproachfully and says without words, 'Too cerebral. Too much head work, old chap. Far too controlled.'

Thank you, monkeys, for inviting the tense, lost child to play, to share your games, to savour your ease. Thank you for asking me not to go to that staircase unprepared, before due time.

This unusual imagery of animal instinct is replaced by a spectacular, noble, white swan descending from the darkened sky, her wings spanned outwards. She's a majestic swan, not a tiny dove.

Then the swan becomes transformed into a white pelican before she reaches earth. A pelican is a self-sacrificing bird who will bleed her breast to give nutrition to her young. Then the bird recedes in flight as if a played-back motion picture, retrograding towards the night sky, flying backwards.

Once more the need for physical, mental, emotional regeneration is emphasised. I hear you, white bird, and I know my work in this parish, set in the hills of Chalatenango, will be winding to a close. This is my seventh year here – the time of completion. Time for ceding the place and taking substantial leisure time is fast approaching. Only after play with the monkeys will I be recharged sufficiently and be able to ascend the red staircase leading to a new phase of work.

THE VILLAGE ALMOND TREE
22nd May 1993

'It's a nice tree that,' says Corina,
nodding beyond church railings.
I see tree's thick foliage spread
from far-stretching brown boughs
casting deep shade and mystery,
protecting weary wayfarers
from bright light of sun's rays.
Verdant and alive, sprouting strong,
proud phallic tree unbowed,
seen daily through house's square window,
refreshing sight that tree.
'Yes,' I agree,
'It's a beautiful, beautiful tree.'

With her smile concealing rage and grief
Corina responds,
'Eleven years gone
the death squad hung till dead my brother
from that tree.'

ODE TO A FAT RAT
19th September 1993 – 1.58am

More chance there was
that scorpions fall from heaven
into my tea cup,
but it happened that
a fat grey rat,
size of a cat,
coat brylcreemed back by rain,
ears pricked alerted,
startled,
fell slap bang thud
through a sodden ceiling
into my darkened bedroom.
Bigger by far than any fish
Henry claimed to catch on Achill Isle,
but much less agile.
'Thou were too slow,
far too slow,
stodgy creature,
vermin fiend.
And the shutter stick
wielded by this primitive hunter
struck thee mortal blows.
Oh woe is thee,
caught in the throes of death,
smashed senseless in uneven combat.
Big, sleekit, quivering bold beastie,
never again visit my warm dry domain
and shelter from night's cold pouring rain.

THE STRUGGLE FOR PEACE
9th November 1993

IN THE CHURCH OF El Rosario, San Salvador, standing before
the grey coffin of her slain husband, the wife of Francisco Véliz,
ex-Commander of the FMLN, took the microphone. Sobbing
with distress, she read out a love letter she had composed to
her dead companion. Journalists drew near, jockeying with
photographers for space; flashbulbs lit up momentarily the array
of coloured wreaths. The woman's words echoed in vain for a
response.

Francisco lay dead, murdered as he circled the rear of his
car, walking to open the farside door and release their two-
year-old girl into her nursery school. The reality is that death
squad murderers are cowards who kill defenceless people,
leaving loved ones of those killed to grieve. Véliz's wife has their
three young children to nourish and support into adulthood.
The family breadwinner is gone forever, a victim of senseless
violence. Since the signing of the peace accord, twenty-five
members of the FMLN political party have been murdered. One
girl who lived in Guazapa was breast-feeding her baby when the
assassin's bullet struck her dead. People are worried and afraid.
The death squad structure is still in operation and their crimes
go unpunished. The FMLN are refraining from retaliation,
realising that to enter into a spiral of violence once again would
serve no purpose. Instead, they have protested to the United
Nations who are observing the peace process and they await the
results of an investigation set up by the FBI, Scotland Yard and
other international police forces present in the country.

President Clinton has agreed to open up classified files from
the United State government's archives. These will, hopefully,
shed light on the identity of the death squad murderers and the
oligarchic figures who provide their financial support.

The United Nation's Truth Commission ought to reconsider

the decision to withhold the names of those promoting death squad murders. They decided not to mention these names in their report in order not to destabilise the nation. This collusion has been one of the factors permitting the situation of impunity to continue and more lives are threatened as a result. Only the truth will set us free.

On 6 November I accompanied a group of fellow parishioners to the Church of San Antonio in the town of Chalatenango. We went there to participate in the fast for peace led by Jon Cortina, Society of Jesus, the Chalatenango Deputy Sandoval, the ebullient María Chichilco and the ex-rebel leader Héctor Martínez. About fifty others were present with them. Our participation was partial. I spent only thirty-six hours without food and felt the pinch of hunger. They continued to fast. Also I found the stone floor of the church a bed hard and cold during the night. This kept me awake as much as hearing the love sighs of intercourse within the darkened building.

The war has ended but peace has not replaced it. The struggle for a new life and a new society continues. Maybe this struggle has no ending in history, nothing is absolute.

1994

FÉLIX'S FINAL JOURNEY
16th January 1994

'"Get on your feet, man, he's calling you." He cast off
his mantle, leapt to his feet, and went to Jesus.'
(Mark 1:49)

No more shall we see
that hat of straw,
that grubby shirt stained,
those overlong trousers bunched at shins
by oversize broken brown boots
as Félix shuffles a slow-motion moonwalk
on an alien planet.
Blinded blue eyes
fish-scaled cataracts,
stick taps time to silent music
and sweeps for mines
under cemented streets.
From house to house
on daily ritual moonwalk
Félix begs food to eat,
charity to survive.
Saturday is our day to donate.
'Give me the Host tomorrow, Padre,'
and his daily bread too.
'Sure, Félix,' I assure him.
As flotsam adrift
this old man knows
a child's need of God's bread.
Early Sunday morning
he sits alone in church and whispers secrets
to the Divinity unseen.
Félix, blind beggar, arise now,

purgatory is over on this alien planet.
Cast aside the mantle of mortality,
the Master bids you come to Him.

ADIÓS,
DANIEL DASTARDLY
(PART 3 OF 3)
15th February 1994

THIS IS TO BE my last evening visiting the community of Los Naranjos. I stand outside the church and chat to three of the men. It's probable that I shall never pass this way again nor shall I ever again meet these people, people whose joys and sorrows I've shared for more than seven years.

Chico and Porfirio take their leave and I find myself alone with Daniel Ardón, his stick and 'corvo' (harvesting sword) are propped against the belfry. The conversation that ensues takes me by surprise. Ardón, his lips perpetually sloping chinward like Brando's Godfather, is crying, his voice tremulous. 'I give thanks to you,' he says, 'and to God for what you did for me.'

Six years ago he was due to be executed by the Guerrilla for espionage. He was searching out the whereabouts of FMLN camps in the hills, was discovered, and detained. His life was spared as a result of a petition signed by the community, at my instigation. These words of thanks were his first acknowledgement of my having saved his life.

'Enjoy life,' I tell him with a smile.

He pulls out his wallet from his pocket, takes a five peso note and hands it to me. I desist from receiving it, but he insists, saying, 'What's given is never lost.'

I look at the note, the equivalent value of fifty pence, and wonder with a touch of black humour if the life of an army spy is worth as much. Yet, secretly, I wish Daniel Ardón years of health and happiness.

'¿QUIÉN COMO DIOS?'
17th February 1994

AS OUR DEPARTURE DATE draws near, certain Franciscan friars in La Palma are telling our parishioners that, after we leave, they intend to come and 'restore the faith' in our communities, because 'faith is dead'.

On hearing these comments I shake my head and smile at clerical hubris. Why is it that we clergy think we possess faith and are going to donate some of it to dim, pagan yokels? The truth is that the people evangelise us with their sense of God and their simple goodness in day to day living, but we're too proud to realise that.

Take old Purificación for example. Every time I arrive in Los Llanitos, he comes to ask for prayer. He doesn't ask for anything else, only prayer. He removes his old hat, bows his bare head and mutters, '¿Quién como Dios?' Who cares more tenderly for us than God? Who with God compares? '¿Quién como Dios?'

Fratres maiores, the people's faith is alive. Learn from them.